MW00785819

Elevating the School Library

Purchases of AASL Publications fund advocacy, leadership, professional development, and standards initiatives for school librarians nationally.

ALA Editions purchases fund advocacy, awareness, and accreditation programs for library professionals worldwide.

Susan D. Ballard
and Sara Kelly Johns

ELEVATING THE SCHOOL LIBRARY

Building Positive Perceptions through Brand Behavior

American Association
of School Librarians
TRANSFORMING LEARNING

CHICAGO | 2024

© 2024 by Susan D. Ballard and Sara Kelly Johns

Extensive effort has gone into ensuring the reliability of the information in this book; however, the publisher makes no warranty, express or implied, with respect to the material contained herein.

ISBN: 978-0-8389-3870-6 (paper)

Library of Congress Cataloging-in-Publication Data

Names: Ballard, Susan D., author. | Johns, Sara Kelly, author.
Title: Elevating the school library : building positive perceptions through brand behavior / Susan D. Ballard and Sara Kelly Johns.
Description: Chicago : ALA Editions, 2024. | Includes bibliographical references and index. | Summary: "A focused exploration of the importance of developing the school library brand in alignment with the AASL Standards, this book emphasizes brand behavior to assist the school librarian in demonstrating the value of the school library and the role of the school librarian"—Provided by publisher.
Identifiers: LCCN 2023016484 | ISBN 9780838938706 (paperback)
Subjects: LCSH: School libraries—United States—Administration. | School libraries—United States—Marketing. | School libraries—Public relations—United States. | Branding (Marketing)
Classification: LCC Z675.S3 B227 2023 | DDC 025.1/978—dc23/eng/20230512
LC record available at https://lccn.loc.gov/2023016484

Book design by Alejandra Diaz in the Utopia Std and Galano typefaces.

♾ This paper meets the requirements of ANSI/NISO Z39.48-1992 (Permanence of Paper).

Printed in the United States of America
28 27 26 25 24   5 4 3 2 1

CONTENTS

ACKNOWLEDGMENTS

We are forever grateful to the many people who assisted us as we undertook this endeavor. We'd like to thank our colleagues across the country who took the time to respond to our survey about school library brand versus personal brand. Although we could not incorporate all your wonderful input, we were happy to include your best thinking to help illuminate the need for a look at branding for the profession.

We are also indebted to several individuals who provided more personal insights regarding branding. Vi Harada, Pam Harland, and Joyce Valenza are true inspirations to us, and we deeply value your contributions.

Where would we be without the generosity of Debbie and Damon Abilock? They allowed us a complimentary subscription to the remarkable NoodleTools to compile our citation list and answered our questions as we grappled with the Chicago style!

Our amazing and extremely patient ALA/AASL editors Stephanie Book and Jamie Santoro were there for us all the way. Their brilliant suggestions and ability to get us to focus when we would tend to ramble cannot be understated.

And last, the entity we have come to know as "Froger"—our all-too-similar, grumpy, curmudgeonly husbands, Roger and Frank. We know it was a long haul—but enough already. Get over it! Seriously, we appreciate your support and how much you value the work we do and our passion for school libraries.

INTRODUCTION
Why This Book?

If you think this book is about "how to develop a logo and a tagline" or how to make yourself a recognized name in school library land, please return it before you crack the spine. But if you have the idea that there is more to school library branding than that, settle in and be prepared to be challenged. We suspect that the tagline and logo will likely emerge later if you want them. Name recognition may also occur. However, we decided to write this book because the specific challenge that we, as a profession, need to address is the importance of developing the school library brand in, of, and by itself in alignment with the *National School Library Standards for Learners, School Librarians, and School Libraries*. This is not a book about creating a personal brand—rather, it is about embracing a brand for the school library and the school librarian.

Throughout the book as we introduce and discuss various terms related to branding, we put them in bold type to underscore their conceptual importance and indicate their inclusion in the glossary. Additionally, every chapter provides a list of guiding questions to assist you in undertaking school library branding, a **rebrand**, or a **brand rehabilitation**.

Overall, we provide a focused exploration of and emphasis on brand behavior—its impact, influence, and integrity—including ways in which to use existing American Association of School Librarians (AASL) personas and develop additional learner personas (such as trauma-sensitive learners, special groups, and nonusers) through a brand audit. We also incorporate the use of data and community demographics analysis to assist the everyday school librarian in improving practice, thus increasing positive perceptions of the impact of our work. We further underscore that the focus is not so much on transforming image as it is on building brand credibility through customer service that is legendary.

Think about how often schools and school libraries have been advised or even admonished to act more like a business, recognizing that stakeholders expect us to provide competent management and effective and efficient use of resources to meet deadlines and produce results. Although we can counter such advice by noting that supporting the individual learning needs of humans who are in various stages of intellectual, physical, social, and emotional development is not like turning out a finite product or service, we are nonetheless in a business—the education/

information business. And to stay in business, we need a solid reputation for positive interactions and return on investments. In business, branding is a critical component of a customer's decision to use a particular service or product. In the digital age, this decision is compounded by other customers' experiences and interactions with a brand, which can make or break that brand. Compliments as well as complaints and opinions about a brand not only are spread by word of mouth but are online and viewable through a simple web search or through a wide variety of social networks. There is no way to simply ignore or dismiss customer dissatisfaction. Transparency and authenticity are the only means to survive and thrive in this digital landscape. All these societal and cultural shifts impact our business space as well. So, though this book is designed to get everyone thinking about the school library brand, we underscore that the focus is not so much on transforming the school library's image as it is on building credibility through ongoing improvement and exemplary brand behavior. To align with and connect to the AASL Standards, we also present and analyze successful and unsuccessful business examples as well as school library examples to provide a framework of reference. We discuss the work of experts in the business and corporate world such as Jim Collins (*Good to Great*, 2001), John Kotter and Holger Rathgeber (*Our Iceberg Is Melting*, 2005), and Seth Godin to assist you in further understanding the importance of the business aspects of the school library.

Above all, however, this book is designed to help move us outside our comfort zone—and that is hard. As AASL past president, well-known researcher, and respected educator Ken Haycock once observed to us, attributing Mark Twain, "No one really likes change except a wet baby." Nonetheless, the competitive, disruptive, innovative nature of the information access and education marketplace must be recognized, and we must be ready to respond through the development of strategic, prioritized action plans that help overcome perceived or real brand barriers. Likewise, we must maintain, expand, and encourage active two-way communication with our stakeholders and acknowledge that they have a say in what happens. We need to figure out a way to make the school library and school librarian undisputedly relevant and essential, or we will be innovated out of existence by someone else who gets it. If we don't embrace this challenge, we may well end up like other relics of the past, with our dusty, fossilized remains on display in a museum where somewhat bemused tourists snap a photo or two and contemplate what we must have been like.

AASL has been striving to grow the *National School Library Standards* brand, of which we are all a part. The organization has worked on brand identity—the visible elements (such as color, design, logotype, name, symbol) that together identify and distinguish the brand in the consumer's or customer's mind—and you may be doing that as well. However, as school librarians, we are always rethinking how to convey who we are and what we do and why both are important to our publics. To compete and remain viable, it is necessary to develop a **name brand** because, as a profession,

- we can help transform learning and community;
- we can provide access to resources that help level the playing field and close the literacy divides—foundational (reading, writing, and meaning making), digital, cultural, media, visual, ethical, data, game, computational, health and financial, and civic;
- we can impact student achievement; and
- we can provide a safe and secure environment for all learners.

So let's begin and consider the opportunities and the possibilities that lie before us. Although we'll glance over our shoulder at the past and lessons learned, our goal is to move forward, with a keen understanding of why and how our brand matters and the determination to ensure that others value it, too.

Brand or Brand Behavior?

A brand is the set of expectations, memories, stories, and relationships that, taken together, account for a consumer's decision to choose one product or service over another.

—Seth Godin (2009)

What do you think of when you hear the term *brand*? Most of us would associate that term with a particular name, **logo, tagline,** and perhaps unique **design elements** that an individual, a company, an association, an organization, or other entity has developed and uses to distinguish itself, or its particular product or service, from others. The term also includes **marketing** and **merchandising** to present and promote the product or service. When all these components are combined, the result is referred to as **brand identity**.

However, brand is much more than identity. This is especially true for school libraries. The school library brand is based on others' expectations about school librarians and school libraries given their experiences at points of contact with us. As a profession we need to work on our brand identity. More importantly, however, school librarians need to concentrate on our **brand behavior** and deliver positive interactions in every encounter with our **target audience**. We need to provide quality products and services, not just say we do.

Branding is often the critical factor in an individual's decision to use or not use a product or service. And particularly in the digital age, user interaction with a brand can make or break it. This interface is referred to as **brand experience**. Jeff Bezos was right on the money when he reportedly observed, "Your brand is what other people say about you when you're not in the room." Praise as well as complaints about a brand are communicated and shared through a variety of websites and social networks. It is just a matter of typing a brand name into a search engine to discover a myriad of reviews and opinions about it. As a result of this participatory societal and cultural shift, it is increasingly difficult, if not impossible, to conceal or obscure customer dissatisfaction. Businesses recognize that technology and communication channels have empowered the average person and that transparency and authenticity are the only means to survive and thrive in a digital environment. This shift has impacted the school library "business" space, too. Although most schools and school libraries are considered nonprofit, make no mistake about it: school libraries are in business—the information and education business—and school librarians need to uphold a solid reputation for positive experiences, interactions, and returns on investments if we are to survive in an increasingly competitive environment.

Unfortunately, school library brand identity has often been shaped by forces outside the profession. The stereotypical image of a librarian projected by the advertising world has what is called **stickiness** in marketing circles—that is, it is an idea so memorable that it stays in the mind of the consumer or end user. "A brand is a psychological construct held in the minds of all those aware of the branded product, person, organization, or movement" (Kylander and Stone 2012). The advertising world's perception of a librarian has had great staying power in the minds of the public. As noted by Gretchen Keer and Andrew Carlos (2015) in *American Libraries*, "There are numerous librarian stereotypes, with the most recognizable being the middle-aged, bun-wearing, comfortably shod, shushing librarian. Others include the sexy librarian, the superhero librarian, and the hipster or tattooed librarian." And as if that is not enough, school librarians are also often up against the user's memory of an underperforming school librarian, or worse yet, lack of memory of ever encountering a school librarian and, therefore, no idea of what should be expected. It is a struggle to change the impression some people have about librarians. So much so that many of us are singularly obsessed with it at times and go all out in our effort to change perceptions—usually by renaming ourselves or trying to stand out from the crowd by concentrating on our personal image instead of elevating the overall image of the profession. After all, "it takes more than a hat to be a cowboy" (Godin 2009). It is as if we think by giving ourselves a new name or being seen as one of the cool kids, we will somehow magically transform into a new and improved version of librarianship without acquiring the requisite skills, competencies, and dispositions that are the hallmark of professionalism. The only way to improve the school library brand is to assess where one is in terms of development and do the work needed to get to the next level. The only audience that school librarians need to impress is the learning community that we serve. So where do we go from here?

Creating a Brand That Sticks

The notion that schools and school libraries are confined to a physical space has been upended for some time now. Just as the business world has evolved to embrace e-commerce and two-way, participatory digital communication to remain relevant, schools and school libraries have likewise needed to adapt to also include a virtual presence and employ both traditional and social media outlets to connect with defined audiences. However, we have not necessarily recognized what the commercial marketplace has always had to contend with—and that is the competitive nature of the landscape in which we now exist. There may have been a time when the provision of learning opportunities, information brokering, and curated collections of resources were the exclusive domain of the formal academic community, but that time is over. Learning and information are everywhere. If you have access to a smartphone, you have free access to a wealth of knowledge provided by a host of experts in almost every discipline via platforms such as YouTube, Khan Academy, and Duolingo. In addition, massive open online courses (MOOCs) provided by individual colleges and universities as well as services such as Blackboard, the Canvas Network, and Coursera allow open access to courses of study, with the option of receiving credit for a reasonable fee. And there are professional development and continuing education providers such as LinkedIn Learning (formerly Lynda) serving certification and recertification needs for licensure requirements. So who needs librarians when in many instances these providers offer credible services and meet the wants and must-haves of their users in an efficient and effective way? How do we convince people that what we provide is indeed different and important to them?

We know that the link between strong school libraries and student achievement is well documented. We also know that

> [g]rounded in standards and best practice, school libraries are an integral component of the educational landscape. The school library provides an environment in which teaching and learning are the primary emphases. The school library provides a space and place for personalized learner success; learners are encouraged to explore questions of personal and academic relevance. Under the direction of a qualified school librarian, school libraries are instrumental in fostering literacy and teaching inquiry skills to support lifelong learning. (AASL 2018b, 54)

The evidence is clear that school librarians and school libraries make a difference. What is needed now is unrelenting focus on attaining that elusive stickiness that comes with **brand loyalty** because when the essential conditions are in place, nobody does it better.

Knowing that the product school librarians and libraries provide is valuable and needed is one thing. The more important question for us is how do we ensure that the library stands out in the noisy space that is the school, where everyone is constantly jockeying for position, support, and resources (Ibrisevic 2019)? The best way to emerge from being boxed in or marginalized is by being memorable and by being intentional in the development of services that address end users' needs and wants. We must focus on user engagement and positive experiences to develop loyalty and trust, knowing that increased engagement will lead to support, funding, and stickiness. Building an effective and memorable brand relies on this baseline understanding of the direction in which your audiences are moving and on ensuring that they understand why you are relevant to the successful achievement of their goals. Remember this phrase: *Every encounter and transaction must support brand expectations.* For school librarians that means our dealings with **stakeholders** must always be positive or redressed to favor the user or provide a learning opportunity.

Brand Perception

As you reflect on your school library brand, consider what your stakeholders currently expect from their perceptions of your brand. First, who is the audience for your brand? Better, who are your audiences? Of course, we think of our learners first, but, to be most effective with our learners, we need to work closely with all stakeholders. Other educators expect us to design and co-teach inquiry collaborative lessons and units, and they count on us for collection development that meets all learners' information and reading needs (AASL 2018b, 60). Parents or guardians want their children to find books in all formats that will excite them to read, have opportunities to develop critical thinking skills, and have access to technology with instruction that will help their children be safe and productive online. Administrators—building principals, school library supervisors (if you are lucky enough to have one), superintendents, business managers—want a school library that is aligned with the district's mission and that is staffed by an expert in literacy, digital and information literacy instruction, collection development, and inclusion. They need an educational leader as their school librarian.

RELEVANCE MATTERS

As [school] librarians, we can offer the very best hammer in the world, but if your principal, your teachers, or your parents really need and want a wrench, a screwdriver, or a hacksaw, having a hammer, no matter how wonderful, is simply immaterial. They get it that you have a great hammer—it just isn't relevant or important to them. Even if you think it darned well should be.

—Doug Johnson, retired school library and technology director, Minnesota (*Blue Skunk Blog*, May 29, 2013)

Perception is everything. Are we seen by our stakeholders as relevant to what they want and need? We want them to perceive that the school librarian and library are crucial to the school and that we offer these benefits:

- Schedules aligned with what works for users, borrowing policies that suit them, policies that make life easier for them, and access that is not controlled just to make the school librarian's life easier.
- Experiences—collaborative projects, literacy instruction, book checkout, student opportunity zones—that support what our users need and expect.
- A positive attitude—"I have a job that makes users' school existence better"— rather than a dismissive attitude—"School libraries exist so I can have a job."
- Flexible partnerships that are for the good of the order due to the mutability of the school's needs, not for the convenience of the librarian (too often the perception).
- School library advisory groups that value input of representatives from the administration team, classroom educators, parents, and learners.
- School librarians who are exceptional and are "exceptioners," with fees and fines waived given special circumstances and policies waived when needed to benefit learners (e.g., a learner being temporarily allowed to eat lunch in the school library to mitigate a bullying problem).
- School librarians who are flexible, approachable, collegial, and valued as teaching partners and essential collaborators—not as babysitters or monitors for classes or an alternative study hall. The school library is seen as a learning environment—your classroom, not a multipurpose room.

What if your school library is perceived instead as being all about books and computers and rules, a closed program stuck on itself instead of being approachable, flexible, and focused on learners' growth? If you strongly suspect that perceptions like these are the case in your school, you have a lot of work ahead to change those perceptions so that stakeholders instead hold expectations of what a strong school library program is and, in turn, what your brand represents. You need to listen; you need to gently nudge stakeholders in the direction that will help learners thrive as you work together. After all, school libraries are not candy stores; they are places where all stakeholders can get a solid meal, *plus* a great dessert! We have standards that show learners and educators what school librarians and libraries can do, and what users can expect. But to take that *good* program to the *great* program that exemplifies your brand requires leadership.

You will need to be—and be perceived as—a leader, a school librarian role first defined by AASL in *Empowering Learners: Guidelines for School Library Programs* (AASL 2009). The addition of this role was an awakening for many school librarians already familiar with the roles of instructional partner, information specialist, teacher, and program administrator. The leadership role was affirmed in the *National School Library Standards for Learners, School Librarians, and School Libraries*:

> The school librarian is "a teacher and a learner who listens to and acts upon good ideas from peers, educators, and learners" (AASL 2018b, 14).

Andy Warhol is often quoted as saying, "Perception precedes reality." It is crucial that your users (learners, educators, staff, community) perceive your leadership as promised by your school library's brand. Leadership will elevate you and your program from "good to great," a business world concept defined by Jim Collins (2001) that works in the library world as well. You can have a really *good* school library program, but if no one knows about it, it will never be a *great* school library program. It takes leadership and hard work to have a great program that lives up to its brand, work that is driven by dedication to the belief that strong school libraries make a difference in the lives of learners.

Leadership and Perception

We can take lessons from the business and the nonprofit worlds and benefit from their expertise in leadership. One of the most highly regarded gurus in this area is the aforementioned Jim Collins, author of *Good to Great* (2001) and *Good to Great and the Social Sectors* (2005). The big takeaway from both books is that there are levels of leadership that contribute to organizations (including school libraries), with the ultimate, most effective leaders being the Level 5 Executives who build "enduring greatness through a paradoxical blend of personal humility and professional will" (Collins 2001, 2005).

Collins developed this leadership hierarchy after his five-year study of successful good-to-great companies uncovered similar characteristics in leaders across all the companies studied—even though his team was not looking for such characteristics. The data showed that leadership mattered, and this hierarchy resulted (figure 1.1). The formula HUMILITY + WILL = LEVEL 5 (Collins 2001, 22) was a constant in the great companies. Collins explained that Level 5 leadership is not only about modesty and humility but also about fierce resolve, the determination to do what needs to be done to make the company great (36). We contend that great school library programs require outstanding school librarians who are humble and have the resolve to do whatever it takes to ensure that their programs meet the needs of everyone in their school communities. The following description sounds exactly

LEVEL 5 | **LEVEL 5 EXECUTIVE**
Builds enduring greatness through a paradoxical blend of personal humility and professional will.

LEVEL 4 | **EFFECTIVE LEADER**
Catalyzes commitment to and vigorous pursuit of a clear and compelling vision, stimulating higher performance standards.

LEVEL 3 | **COMPETENT MANAGER**
Organizes people and resources toward the effective and efficient pursuit of pre-determined objectives.

LEVEL 2 | **CONTRIBUTING TEAM MEMBER**
Contributes individual capabilities to the achievement of group objectives and works effectively with others in a group setting.

LEVEL 1 | **HIGHLY CAPABLE INDIVIDUAL**
Makes productive contributions through talent, knowledge, skills, and good work habits.

FIGURE 1.1
Level 5 hierarchy

Source: Collins 2001. Reprinted by permission of Curtis Brown, Ltd. All rights reserved..

like the people in the school library profession whose programs are regarded as indispensable in their school districts:

> Level 5 leaders channel their ego needs away from themselves and into the larger goal of building a great company. It's not that Level 5 leaders have no ego or self-interest. Indeed, they are incredibly ambitious—*but their ambition is first and foremost for the institution, not themselves.* (Collins 2001, 21, emphasis in original)

In fact, when we asked in a survey how she developed her school library brand in relation to her school/program, its needs, and its culture, school librarian and Level 5 leader Iris Eichenlaub responded, "My job is to constantly assess and adapt and respond to the needs and interests of our community. If the library is exactly the same in five years, I am not fulfilling my mandate" (Eichenlaub, survey response to authors, 2021).

Sometimes moving from good to great feels hard because of the introverted personalities of a large percentage of school librarians (an anecdotal conclusion from our years of experience in the profession). However, you can "flip the switch" (Johns

---

Summary: The Two Sides of Level 5 Leadership

Professional Will	**Personal Humility**
Creates superb results, a clear catalyst in the transition from good to great.	Demonstrates a compelling modesty, shunning public adulation, never boastful.
Demonstrates an unwavering resolve to do whatever must be done to produce the best long-term results, no matter how difficult.	Acts with quiet, calm determination; relies primarily on inspired standards, not inspiring charisma, to motivate.
Sets the standard of building an enduring great company; will settle for nothing less.	Channels ambition into the company, not the self; sets up successors for even greater success in the next generation.
Looks in the mirror, not out the window, to apportion responsibility for poor results, never blaming other people, external factors, or bad luck.	Looks out the window, not in the mirror, to apportion credit for the success of the company—to other people, external factors, and good luck.

FIGURE 1.2

Summary: The two sides of Level 5 leadership

Source: Collins 2001. Reprinted by permission of Curtis Brown, Ltd. All rights reserved..

2015, 169) when you conclude that you are providing and promoting a program that can give learners the chance to graduate ready for college, a career, and life. It's not about you per se; it's about the school library. You can do it. You may have downplayed your leadership qualities, but they are there—and it is worth the time and effort to move yourself up that leadership hierarchy. You will need to assess, reflect, seek professional development opportunities, develop a personal learning network, and promote/market the strengths of your library, your brand.

Figure 1.2 is a visual depiction of this Collins quote: "To spot a Level 5 leader, look for situations where extraordinary results exist but where no individual steps forth to claim excess credit—humility" (Collins 2001, 36).

User Engagement and Personas

Although you may think that you have too much else to do and don't have the time to focus on developing and maintaining a brand (it is hard work and time-consuming), the result pays long-term dividends in terms of increased awareness, understanding, commitment to and support of your work and your value to the school. A strong brand is "critical in helping to build operational capacity, galvanize support, and maintain focus on the social mission" (Kylander and Stone 2012).

Consider, and answer, the following questions as the foundation to shape your school library brand's development. Revisit these questions often to stay true to your brand:

- Is this school library welcoming? Welcoming to everybody?
- What is our message?
- What is our style?
- How do we listen?
- Is this a school library I would like to use as a learner or educator? (adapted from Barber and Wallace 2010)

Start by reviewing the mission/vision of both the school and the library. Specifically, consider the raison d'etre of the school library as it relates to the mission/vision of the school. The school library is there to serve the school. It is a part of the school, not a separate institution. Solicit stakeholders for their input and assess the environment to better understand the community served (Ibrisevic 2019).

These strategies will help you begin building profiles of your audiences and understand who you are working for. AASL took a page from the business world when the organization incorporated personas in the development and implementation of the *National School Library Standards*. This is a marketing strategy that you can also use to help create organizational cohesion and build capacity. We'll take a deeper dive into the use of personas in chapter 2.

Questions for the Reflective Practitioner

1. Now that you have read this chapter, reconsider the first sentence: "What do you think of when you hear the term *brand*?"

2. What does your school library offer that is unique and needed or desired by your stakeholders?

3. What elements of your school library brand do you think have achieved stickiness with your current brand loyalists?

4. If perception precedes reality, how do you think your administrator perceives your school library? Your educators? Your learners?

5. How do you become a Level 5 leader? What if you currently see yourself as a Level 4 or even a Level 3 leader?

Lessons from the Business World

People do things for their reasons, not yours. Find theirs.
—*Dale Carnegie (1981)*

Who is Noah Who Needs Support? Inez the Innovator? Margot the Mentor? Athena the Academic? Leon the Lead Learner? Tony the Teacher? Patty the Parent? Why are they so prominent in the *National School Library Standards*? Are they based on real people? Well . . . kind of.

As school librarians received their copy of the *National School Library Standards for Learners, School Librarians, and School Libraries*, their most frequent thought was likely, where do I start? How do I work with these standards with my students (learners) and teachers (classroom educators) to make a difference? Thumbing through the first chapter, readers found silhouette graphics of people depicting "personas." These personas were developed by the AASL Standards and Guidelines Implementation Task Force as the members sought to design a marketing plan and support materials for school librarians who would use the AASL Standards to guide and encourage students' deep learning (AASL 2018b, 20–24). Inspired by the work she was doing with her library and information science (LIS) students at Rutgers University, task force member Joyce Valenza shared with the task force a persona business theory relating to strategic planning and website creation:

> Heavily used in the design community, personas are a research-based strategy that helps build understandings of the needs and behaviors of communities served. They add human focus to design and innovation solutions. Personas are used to help design thinkers move from the Empathy phase to the Ideation phase and to facilitate continual improvements. (Valenza, e-mail interview by Sara Kelly Johns, December 11, 2020)

The task force agreed that knowing the audiences to whom AASL was marketing these standards was vital to developing more meaningful implementation resources. The task force wanted answers to these questions:

- Who would be the users of the AASL Standards?
- Who would implement the AASL Standards right away?
- Who might need help in implementing the AASL Standards?
- What other people besides school librarians would benefit from the AASL Standards?

A user-centered design allowed the task force to understand AASL audiences through broad profiles, or **personas**. "The Standards implementation task force constructed character profiles to represent different groups who share similar traits, beliefs, attitudes, and values with regard to school libraries" (AASL 2018b, 20). As the AASL Standards were written and the implementation strategies developed, the persona profiles enabled discussion among the working groups about what Noah would need to grow his school library or what Tony would find within the AASL Standards to inspire or energize collaboration with Inez.

One of the universal dispositions of school librarians is that we are lifelong learners, as well as good researchers. Give school librarians a problem to solve and we will define the information need, conduct a thorough search using suitable sources, evaluate what we find by matching the results to the defined need, and curate the best sources to find the best solution. As you begin your path to developing or revisiting a school library brand that reflects your effectiveness and ever-evolving roles, be mindful that too many administrators and classroom educators do not realize all the support and leadership that is already available to them through you. In the September/October 2020 issue of *Knowledge Quest*, Melanie Lewis discussed her doctoral research into why there is a need for school librarians to perpetually advocate for themselves and their school libraries. She concluded that "lack of knowledge and understanding of the instructional role of the school librarian has prevented many administrators from working with their school librarians to provide professional learning within daily instructional practice" (48). Groan. That needs to change! How can we better understand and work with Leon the Lead Learner? How can we better understand and serve all our stakeholders?

User-Centered Design

School libraries can't and shouldn't be run exactly like businesses, but we can learn from the business world and adapt its tools to focus the work we do and transform perceptions through building a strong brand. A business best practice that school libraries can adapt is user-centered design, which correlates well with librarians' reflection on their users: "User experience (UX) focuses on having a deep understanding of users, what they need, what they value, their abilities, and also their limitations . . . UX best practices promote improving the quality of the user's interaction with and perceptions of your product and any related services" (U.S. General Services Administration, n.d.). Developing a user-centered brand (not a tagline or logo; those come later in the process) starts with investigating who our users are—and what they need and want from our school library and its programs. Using UX, we can begin to address the misperceptions of administrators that Lewis found in her dissertation study and improve our brand identity and value.

Empathy is a crucial disposition for school librarians as we go through this process—school librarians need to empathize with users' needs, frustrations, and situations. To develop a brand that reflects the value of what our school libraries provide for our users, we may want to consider using Peter Morville's "User Experience Honeycomb" (figure 2.1) as a measure of how well we are addressing user experience. Morville (2004) examined the design of an effective website as his focus; school librarians examine the perceptions, effectiveness, and value of our school libraries, and our brand reflects that focus.

Transposing the honeycomb's visual message for web design to that of a user-centered school library is a one-to-one correlation. The figure's six measures are

FIGURE 2.1
User experience honeycomb

Source: Morville 2004.

applicable to school libraries that are user-centered, whether that user is a kindergarten learner in the library with a class to find and sign out just the right book; a new classroom educator taking the first steps of a collaborative learning experience; a senior doing research for a capstone project; or an administrator discovering the power of a school librarian teaching safe and meaningful use of digital resources. Suzanne Sannwald, school librarian in San Diego's Grossmont Union High School District, worked in a corporate setting for two years prior to becoming a school librarian. She found that the UX design in Morville's honeycomb formed a basis for UX design in her school library. Sannwald found that library experiences were more meaningful for her learners when she listened to them, modifying her practices to reflect their needs. Her five tips for improving learner experience led her to a turnaround in the focus of her user design: "No matter how much training and experience we may have, we must design our school libraries with our users at the center. It is not about us being wrong, but about making our libraries work right for users" (Sannwald 2017, 47). She suggests:

1. Listen to yourself.
2. Listen to your users.
3. Be explicit.
4. Avoid being overly explicit.
5. Start your perpetual beta now.

Sannwald's hints for school librarians, especially the last hint with its reference to a "perpetual beta," suggest that any design we develop for our school library must be centered on the user, constantly evaluated, and changed as our stakeholders' needs evolve. UX provides school librarians a process to keep our libraries responsive and accountable.

Personas and the Change Process

There are myriad ways to integrate the user-centered thinking depicted in Morville's honeycomb into the creative process of UX design for school libraries. "Personas are one of the most effective ways to empathize with and analyze users during the design process" (Goltz 2014). Empathy with the needs and wants of users (needs and wants that are often, but not always, the same) can confirm strategic directions for our school library that we may have already concluded, but it may also help us realize that our intuition and training are imperfect and not always what we should follow when creating a user-centered program. We need to know who our stakeholders are and what matters to them. In *Smashing Magazine*, interaction designer and user researcher Schlomo "Mo" Goltz reinforced the importance of personas: "An effective way to gain knowledge of, build empathy for, and sharpen focus on users is to use a persona" (Goltz 2014). When creating personas, survey your library users to gain a better understanding of their needs. Goltz offered this advice for the questions you ask:

- Ask primarily open-ended questions.
- Ask participants to show more than tell.
- When possible, ask for specific stories, especially about anything you cannot observe. (2014)

Personas are usually created by businesses and marketers during the planning process to act as representatives of the users who will buy their product or effectively use their service. "The theory is that designers should think about personas as if they were real people, referring to their names, imaging [sic] conversations with them, and advocating for their interests" (Humphrey 2017, 13; see also Ward 2010). Personas are also useful for evaluation later in the process, holding the designers accountable for authentic use and potential change. Alan Cooper, who developed this concept of personas, explained that "personas are not real people, but they are based on the behaviors and motivations of real people we have observed and represent them throughout the design process" (Cooper, Riemann, and Cronin 2007, 75). A now-archived Usability.gov guide provides an incredibly useful description for understanding personas—something that should be part of everyone's repertoire. The guide defines effective personas as those who:

- Represent a major user group for your website
- Express and focus on the major needs and expectations of the most important user groups
- Give a clear picture of the user's expectations and how they're likely to use the site
- Aid in uncovering universal features and functionality
- Describe real people with backgrounds, goals, and values (usability.gov/how-to-and -tools/methods/personas.html)

For school librarians developing our brand using personas, we would substitute the word *library* for the word *website* in the first bullet point to start our process.

Taking a closer look at the personas developed by AASL may help reveal the value of personifying representational groups that would be affected by the AASL Standards. AASL stated that "our personas are designed to cut across categories of stakeholders and unify them into fewer, but clearly defined, user groups that we want to reach with the standards" (AASL 2018b, 20). The AASL Standards Implementation Task Force knew that AASL members as well as other stakeholders would be aware of the AASL Standards if not already using them, but the task force members questioned how the standards would "touch" each group. To explore this question, task force members Valenza and Johns identified several groups of librarians and stakeholders who shared similar traits and attitudes, specifically exploring their perceptions of school libraries before being introduced to the AASL Standards. As the task force further refined these portraits and considered the standards in action, the personas facilitated opportunities to have user-centered discussions about the standards and materials to support implementation. By referring to each persona with a mnemonic device name, task force members were able to give a voice to the unique needs of school librarians and stakeholders while evaluating the effectiveness and value of the AASL Standards and implementation resources. How does Noah Who Needs Support find that support in the AASL Standards as he convinces Tony the Teacher to collaborate on a new project? Will Inez the Innovator find areas in the AASL Standards that drive her personal growth to lead her already thriving program even further? What tools or resources can AASL provide to support Margot the Mentor in her quest to convince Leon the Lead Learner to advocate for more collaborative planning time for librarians and educators?

AASL and school librarians have continued to demonstrate the usefulness of the personas for professional development relating to the *National School Library Standards* and to apply them to important aspects of the school library and programming. Available on the AASL Standards web portal (standards.aasl.org), AASL's *Developing Inclusive Learners and Citizens Activity Guide* was designed to help school librarians develop inclusive learning communities, and themselves as professionals, through scenarios, activities, and resources focused on "global learning, tolerance, empathy, and equity" (American Library Association [ALA] 2019). Produced by a 2019 ALA Emerging Leaders team, the guide is built on the AASL Standards Shared Foundation of Include and organized by the frameworks

LORENZO **the Learner**

What happens in the library?

Job Title: Learner

AASL Connections: None **Yet**

FIGURE 2.2
Lorenzo the Learner

Source: Mackley and Brackbill 2020. Reprinted with permission from Pennsylvania School Library Association.

for Learners, School Librarians, and School Libraries through the four Domains of Think, Create, Share, and Grow. In it, you will again meet Inez the Innovator and will be introduced to Jennifer the second-year middle school librarian as well as Paola, an English language learner and elementary school student from Guatemala who works with librarian Helen, and other new personas who give life to the guide's scenarios. Emerging Leaders teams have since continued to develop activity guides each year built on the Shared Foundations and utilizing professional learning scenarios that feature AASL personas.

The Pennsylvania School Librarians Association (PSLA) was awarded a 2019 AASL Past-Presidents Planning Grant for *National School Library Standards* and worked intensely to design and produce a webinar to support participants as they implemented AASL's *National School Library Standards* (2018b). PSLA also developed an online course to explore the standards. PSLA knew this approach would meet the needs of their members in a large state where professional development presented at the regional level reaches many more school librarians. When the pandemic forced everyone to work online, these materials were even more effective. The subsequent blog post in *Knowledge Quest* about the PSLA design process and resources connects the existing AASL Standards personas to the Domains (Think, Create, Share, Grow), critical educational initiatives, and excellent digital tools from AASL's Best Digital Tools for Teaching and Learning (Mackley and Brackbill 2020). In addition, PSLA followed the AASL persona model to create two new personas that helped illuminate the power of the AASL Standards for teaching and learning. Meet Lorenzo the Learner (figure 2.2) and Carina the Community Member (figure 2.3)!

CARINA the Community Member

How can I create partnerships with local educational institutions?

Job Title: Local Business Owner

AASL Connections: None **Yet**

FIGURE 2.3

Carina the Community Member

Source: Mackley and Brackbill 2020.
Reprinted with permission from
Pennsylvania School Library Association.

Try This!

Get started by looking at the AASL and PSLA persona examples and thinking about the people you work with and for whom you would be designing services that create the school library's brand—administrators, other educators, staff, learners, parents, school board members, community members. Can you create categories of people with similar attitudes about the school library? Now select two to five people who are similar and use the empathy map (figure 2.4) to explore their wants and needs. Then we will use a persona template to transform your group into a composite persona representative of several people in the same category.

Together, let's create a persona for learners who have a physical disability—specifically, elementary learners who use wheelchairs. Our first step would be to identify two to three learners who use wheelchairs, then complete empathy maps for those learners either through actual interviews with them or through observation and speculation. "An empathy map is a collaborative visualization used to articulate what we know about a particular type of user. It externalizes knowledge about users in order to 1) create a shared understanding of user needs, and 2) aid in decision making" (Gibbons 2018). Analysis of the empathy maps can then merge into a composite persona, very useful as you design your brand and again as you

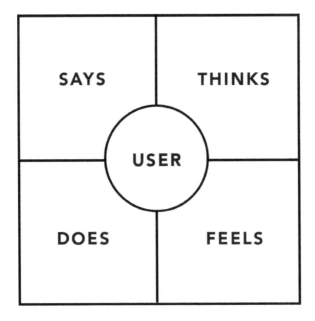

EMPATHY MAP

SAYS   THINKS

USER

DOES   FEELS

FIGURE 2.4

Empathy map   Source: Nielsen Norman Group (nngroup.com).

evaluate and evolve. The learners themselves can fill out the empathy maps, or you can interview the learners. With all your stakeholders, it is necessary to understand who they are and what their needs are—quite true for active learners who must use wheelchairs for mobility.

How would second-grader Lila fill in the empathy map in an interview?

Lila SAYS: I love going to school and Library is my favorite class.

Lila FEELS: I can be just like everyone else in the class when I choose a book because the books I like are on shelves I can reach. It is hard to check out my book at the circulation desk, though. It's too high. Someone must help me.

Lila THINKS: I hope I can be the first one to take out the latest new book, but someone else might get there first because I am not fast getting around the furniture to reach the books.

Lila DOES: I know! I will ask the librarian to put my name on the book I want and save it for me!

Fifth-grader Jack is reluctant to be interviewed, but then opens up by the time he gets to his DOES statement:

Jack SAYS: I like using the computers in the library best.

Jack FEELS: Some of the kids think I am not as smart as they are just because I must be in a wheelchair. It's a good thing that they like my jokes.

Jack THINKS: I wish there were more graphic novels in the library and that my teacher was OK with me using them for book reports. The librarian lets me take graphic novels out to read just because I like them.

Jack DOES: I like to race other kids in the halls because I can go really fast when the teachers aren't looking. I can't do that in the library. Ha-ha!

Fourth-grader Mina fills in her own empathy map:

Mina SAYS: When I go to the library, I like to do group projects.

Mina FEELS: Most of the time in the library, I forget my chair is different from the other kids' chairs while working on projects until it's time to go to my next class.

Mina THINKS: My favorite subject is science, and the library has lots of books about how bodies work.

Mina DOES: Today I am using a computer in the library to try to find stories about girls like me. My librarian will help me if we don't have them. She will know how to get them.

Looking at the three learners' empathy maps and analyzing what they have told us, we can take the next step of developing a composite persona using the School Library Branding Persona Template we adapted after looking at many good marketing and design examples (appendix A). The learners' empathy maps tell us that

- all three learners would like to feel more like everyone else,
- Mina and Jack like using the school library computers,
- Mina and Lila know they can get help from the school librarian when they need it,
- Jack wants more graphic novels whereas Mina would like more books about student learners like her, and
- the physical layout of the school library makes a difference for all three learners.

With our research and data, we move beyond our intuition about school library services for learners who are mobility impaired to develop our persona by using our template to illustrate our group—learners with a disability. We will give this persona

- a name (AASL used a mnemonic device; don't name your persona after anyone you actually know or after a celebrity),
- a gender identity,
- a quote about what is important to that persona,
- an image that will represent your composited persona,
- demographic details such as their role within the learning community, educational background, ethnicity, age group, technology proficiency, and other demographics that matter to your school library,
- a learning variability,
- personality characteristics including priorities/goals, frustrations, and motivations, and
- a brief scenario about what the persona expects from your school library.

Figure 2.5 demonstrates how you may interpret the learners' empathy maps to populate the persona profile template illustrating this learner group.

We would continue with selecting another group of stakeholders—reluctant/struggling readers; non-native English speakers; accelerated learners who need enrichment resources to keep them interested in school, learning at their own pace; classroom educators who emphasize Guided Inquiry; other educators who don't know where the library actually is; administrators who are supportive (or not); school board members; community members who want to support increasing literacy in the town; and others who hope to find a strong library program that is responsive to their needs. Consider these stakeholders with empathy and develop personas to help guide you in planning for your school library—and your brand.

Persona Profile: Dani Differently Abled

SCENARIO

Dani loves her school library visits and pays attention to what the school librarian can do to get her the books and reference resources she needs and wants. Her very favorite books have characters who are also in wheelchairs. She is facing another surgery and recovery that will get her closer to walking one day; she hopes that she will still be able to go to school online and read a lot of books at home.

Name: Dani
Role: Third-grade learner

> "Using a wheelchair does not make me 'different.' I am a regular kid."

DEMOGRAPHICS

Gender Identity: Female

Age Group: 8 years old

Ethnicity: Latina

Education: Grade 3 Honors student

PERSONALITY

- bubbly
- sensitive
- determined
- good sense of humor
- concentrates on schoolwork well
- likes to please other students and her teachers
- comfortable with herself most of the time

PASSIONS

Crafts, music, reading, writing stories, art, iPad games

PRIORITIES/GOALS

Wants to get good grades and be treated like everyone else.

FAVORITE BOOKS

In My Sissy's Wheelchair

By Abbie Luckett Benjamin

The Chance to Fly

By Ali Stroker & Stacy Davidowicz

Song for a Whale

By Lynn Kelly

TECHNOLOGY LEVEL

Uses a computer for research and schoolwork; loves her iPad

LEARNING VARIABILITY

Sometimes has to work at home after surgeries

FRUSTRATIONS

Frustrated with the physical limitations of her wheelchair

MOTIVATIONS

Physical therapy has made hard work the norm; she wants to walk one day

FIGURE 2.5

Persona profile: Dani Differently Abled

Persona Vision

Once you have developed your school library's group of personas (five or six are enough), you are ready to consider your library through your own persona vision. Persona vision, as defined by academic librarians Holt Zaugg and Scott Rackham (2016), refers to seeing your services and products through the eyes of library personas. Personas give you the opportunity to note parts of your school library that meet the needs of your stakeholders—and those parts that need work. For instance, can you adapt pandemic best practices to nimbly provide hybrid library service to the learners who are there in your school library while also including Dani as she recovers from surgery? If not, what equipment do you need to purchase and how do you provide book delivery for Dani and other remote learners? How does your brand reflect that flexibility and inclusion? Follow up on the changes you choose to make after you reimagine your school library. Give yourself a month and then reevaluate: are you living up to that new brand and the needs of your personas?

School librarians lead vital and important programs and services and must exhibit leadership and willingness to change and adapt those programs and services to meet the needs of the times and of the learning community. School librarians can learn about the evolution of brand behavior through combining the use of design thinking, user experience, and personas with the process of change management. John Kotter and Holger Rathgeber's seminal work, *Our Iceberg Is Melting*, provides invaluable guidance for this process, which can help facilitate change in school libraries much as it has done in the business community. Kotter and Rathgeber emphasized the need for the following actions:

- Set the stage—create a sense of urgency.
- Pull together a guiding group—make sure there is a powerful, diverse group guiding the change.
- Decide what to do—develop the change vision and strategy; clarify how the future will be different from the past.
- Make it happen—communicate for understanding; make sure that as many people as possible understand and accept the vision and strategy.
- Don't let up—press harder and faster after the first success.
- Make it stick—create a new culture and hold on to the new way of behaving.
- Prepare to deal with resistance—lead through resistance and lack of understanding (e.g., Responsive [Flex] scheduling).

As we conclude this chapter, we salute AASL, the ALA Emerging Leaders, and PSLA for adapting the business best practice of using personas to guide school librarians as they evolve, developing programs and services that are relevant and meaningful for their stakeholders.

Questions for the Reflective Practitioner

1 Thinking about Morville's honeycomb, is your school library user-centered? Would your users characterize the school library and the information and resources there as useful, usable, desirable, findable, accessible?

2 Can you identify five types of users (not five people) in your learning community that you could develop into personas?

3 What group of stakeholders is your first priority to personify in working to develop your school library brand?

Development of a Service Culture

My shorthand definition of a service culture is one where employees are obsessed with customer service.

—Jeff Toister (2018)

Now that you have a better understanding of how the business world uses the concept of personas to appreciate the characteristics and needs of their clientele, let's take a closer look at how the business world applies its learning to the development of a service culture.

Essentially, a **service culture** is one in which the focus is on developing overwhelmingly positive relationships with individual customers. This concept is often difficult for Pre-K–12 educators, including school librarians, to integrate owing to the very nature of the institution of the school and that of libraries. School librarians and other educators purport to want to address each and every child's individual learning needs, yet we often get overinvested in rules and regulations designed to serve the adults in the school and maintain an orderly environment. It can be argued that one of the purposes of education is to ensure that youngsters learn about societal norms and expectations, so there is a need for protocols, procedures, and boundaries. But for our purposes, let's leave the restrictions of this habitat for a bit and look at the business ecosystem for some examples of an approach to service culture that we might be able to adapt.

A Business World Example

One of Susan's favorite examples of how a service culture is established and flourishes involves her becoming a total devotee of an American business icon—Nordstrom. Being New Hampshire born and bred, Susan did not have Nordstrom, a West Coast concern, on her radar until, by total serendipity, well-known LIS professor, researcher, and library fashionista David Loertscher introduced her to this venerable institution. Many, many years ago when Susan was still young and foolish enough to wear high heels, she found herself in severe foot distress and unable to walk at an AASL conference. She had been at an off-site meeting and David, gentleman that he is, while accompanying her on a painful walk back to the AASL conference center, exclaimed, "Look, there's Nordstrom! They'll help us!"

Susan had never heard of Nordstrom and wondered if it was some sort of emergency triage center. Imagine her surprise when they walked into a major department store. She wondered why David thought this place would be of any help. Later she learned that Nordstrom started as a shoe store and to this day the main entrance always leads to the shoe department. Within seconds a Nordstrom salesclerk appeared. Exuding great confidence, David said, "This young lady needs your help," and he left her in the clerk's care, which was initially quite puzzling to Susan. The clerk conducted a "reference interview" and, realizing that Susan was a school librarian and not very wealthy, found a pair of very affordable yet absolutely darling shoes. The clerk bent the shank of the shoes to ensure that they would fit without pain and sent Susan on her way. David had been right. The staff at Nordstrom not only were of great help but were happy to oblige. Susan has been a fan of Nordstrom ever since—she still has the shoes! One of her favorite books is *The Nordstrom Way to Customer Service Excellence*, which explains how Nordstrom strives to ensure that work-a-day employees are empowered to make decisions based on the philosophy that Nordstrom wants to cultivate customers for life, not just a single transaction. Initially Susan wondered if it was just a fluke that a Nordstrom employee went out of her way to assist, but she soon found out that this is Nordstrom's corporate culture. In fact, whenever Susan shares her story, listeners invariably chime in with their own positive experiences with Nordstrom. A colleague noted that when she and her husband attended an ALA Midwinter Meeting in Seattle—home of Nordstrom's flagship store—they arrived too early to check into their hotel and were lugging two large suitcases around the streets of the city. Seeing Nordstrom and remembering how accommodating Susan said the staff were, the couple figured they might be welcome to come in and browse, suitcases and all. Not only were they welcomed, but upon learning their circumstances, a sales associate asked if the couple would like to store their suitcases while shopping there, or elsewhere, and retrieve the luggage when it was convenient.

The book *The Nordstrom Way* provides an apprenticeship of sorts as it takes a reader through the development of a customer-driven culture that leads to sustainable, long-term dividends in terms of brand loyalty and support. As one Nordstrom manager observes, "Every time a customer comes into our store it is an opportunity to create a memory" (Spector and McCarthy 2012, 73). The same must hold true for our school libraries. Every transaction with a learner, educator, administrator, parent, or community member is an opportunity to create a positive memory. As we consider how "brand" is the way in which individuals and groups must behave to earn their desired reputation, we need to ask ourselves this question in relation to school libraries and the digital age—what would Nordstrom do?

KICKED OUT OF THE LIBRARY

Consider this cautionary tale from Pam Harland (2014), New Hampshire school library educator. She shares a library encounter that illustrates the need to identify and overcome the barriers and mindsets often held by too many of our customers due to past personal experiences with libraries. The name of the library (and community) has been redacted, but the story is true, and it happened in the not-too-distant past.

––––––––––––––––––

Last week I went to the public library with a colleague to work on a project for our high school. We needed Internet access, a table to spread our documents out on, an outlet to plug in our devices, a spot away from the distractions of our school, and a buzzing atmosphere where we would feel inspired to create new ideas for our project. What better place than the local library?

We arrived to find a very still and silent library. As we walked in, two women behind the main desk glanced at us and then went back to work. Patrons were sitting in chairs reading newspapers. There were some available study carrels in the corners. No group tables near outlets. We tried the second floor. We were faced with several empty chairs and study carrels and signs reading, "No talking." There was an empty "meeting room" with no table and no chairs. Another meeting room was locked.

Because it was 10 a.m., we went into the Teen Room (located directly behind the Reference desk). The room was empty because it was Friday and all the teens in town were in school. We sat at a booth with an outlet and spread out our documents. As soon as we started working, we were interrupted by a staff member who said that we were not allowed to work in there because we would intimidate the teens. I jokingly suggested that the fact that we are high school teachers/librarians could gain us access to this empty room. The librarian did not think my comment was funny and asked us to leave. I asked her for a suggestion of a location where we could work together at a table near an outlet. She said there were

(continued)

outlets all over the walls but could think of no table near an outlet. She recommended we try the second floor, and I said that we would need to talk about our project. She reminded us that we were not allowed to talk on the second floor.

We packed up and spent the day at a local cafe where we sat on couches around a coffee table near an outlet, surrounded by the buzz of the cafe. A young woman was reading a book next to us. An older man was typing hurriedly on his laptop on the other side. People were having meetings, drinking coffee, and getting business done. We were welcomed by the staff. They made us tea. And we got our work done.

Although this example illustrates what went wrong in one public library setting—and even though there are many enlightened librarians who would never allow this sort of situation to occur—we can all visualize something similar occurring in a school library, because the fact of the matter is that it does happen. Essentially, not only is the learner/customer made to feel unwelcome but rules are in place that seem capricious at best and most definitely designed for the benefit of the staff, not the learner.

Consistency of User Experience

Unlike Nordstrom, where there is a conscious and deliberate strategy across stores nationally to ensure the consistency of user experience with the brand, the same is not necessarily true for encounters in school libraries. This is an area in which each school librarian must commit to providing a base level of consistency in the delivery of programs and services to our learning communities. That commitment begins with an understanding of the need to

- implement AASL's *National School Library Standards for Learners, School Librarians, and School Libraries,*
- optimize the use of research and best practice, and
- pursue ongoing professional development and education.

Although there are many challenges to achieving all these goals, which we will address in later chapters, each of us must focus on the need to educate our communities about the baseline standard for school libraries and how our users can assist us in the effort to evolve our school libraries from baseline good to great!

Evolved Public Library Brands

There are many examples in Libraryland of successful branding and rebranding of a library. In terms of public libraries, the esteemed Boston Public Library, or the BPL as it is known by locals, is a great place to start. BPL is on the National Register of Historic Places. The library opened in 1852 as the first free, publicly supported municipal library in America. But the BPL has not stood still or rested on its laurels. As of 2023, it was number seven on Tripadvisor's "Top Attractions in Boston." That's right. Although Fenway Park still rules the roost, Tripadvisor's users consistently sing the praises of the BPL, rating it just below the Boston Tea Party Ships and Museum but above the John F. Kennedy Presidential Museum and Library. It outranks the Samuel Adams Brewery, the Boston Common, the USS *Constitution* (aka *Old Ironsides*), and the Old North Church! Why? Because it is a welcoming, vibrant locus of learning and literacy where all adult residents of the Commonwealth are entitled to borrowing and research privileges (figure 3.1 on the following page). Combine that with free museum passes, concerts in the courtyard, an exciting children's room (with a StoryScape area, sensory learning wall, and kid-friendly interactive technology), a Tween area, and Teen Central (an urban-inspired space with diner-type booths, a digital lab, and a video game lounge), and what's not to like? Add to all that a cafe and the Courtyard Restaurant (which also hosts a great high-tea service), as well as world-class exhibits and more than ten thousand public programs a year, and you get a picture of the consistency of user experience that draws almost 3.6 million visitors a year to the main library and its twenty neighborhood branches.

Another evolved library program is that of the 4th Floor of the Chattanooga Public Library (CPL), described as "a public laboratory and educational facility with a focus on information, design, technology, and the applied arts. . . . [I]t supports the production, connection, and sharing of knowledge by offering access to tools and instruction" (CPL, n.d.). In other words, the 4th Floor is a participatory innovation zone and makerspace developed with user input from what was once a storage area. The emphasis is on service to members of the public as they utilize the creative space and resources. Library personnel, in collaboration with their users, also organize a variety of classes and training programs that address the needs and wants of their clientele. Even in the midst of the COVID-19 pandemic, CPL ensured that the 4th Floor was expressing its service culture: the executive director announced that "after researching what was needed and who was organizing efforts with local

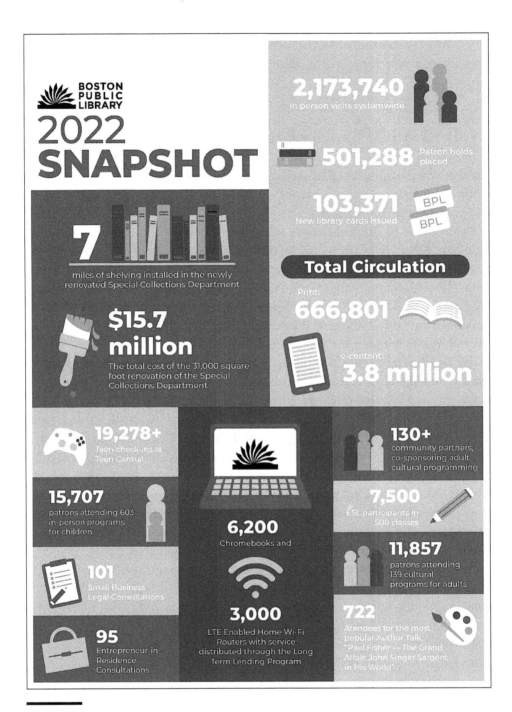

FIGURE 3.1

Boston Public Library 2022 snapshot

Source: BPL 2022.

health care providers, we have teamed up with the Public Education Foundation to produce mask and shield parts with our 3D printers" (Sacco 2020).

It's not just Boston and Chattanooga or urban-centered libraries that are on the bandwagon to evolve their brand. A *New York Times* article entitled "Breaking Out of the Library Mold, in Boston and Beyond" highlights additional examples of how libraries are stepping up to relevancy and to the infusion of a service culture and user experience: "The Lopez Island Library in Washington State offers musical instruments for checkout. In upstate New York, the Library Farm in Cicero, part of the Northern Onondaga Public Library, lends out plots of land on which patrons can learn organic growing practices" (Seelye 2014).

Dynamic School Library Brands

As noted in the beginning of this chapter, sometimes schools have protocols, procedures, rules, and expectations that might limit the level of innovation that school librarians can subscribe to in development of their own service culture and subsequent responsiveness to the needs and wants of the learning community. However, we can (and do) share best practice and success stories with one another through our professional associations and networks. We can also step up to the development of a more consistent user experience by acknowledging and adhering to the implementation of AASL's *National School Library Standards*. Through its National School Library of the Year (NSLY) Award Program, AASL provides a blueprint for measuring the effectiveness of a school library when it honors those school libraries exemplifying the implementation of the AASL Standards. Even if you know that your school library and brand need work, looking at the criteria for the award can help you assess strengths and weaknesses and begin to plan for a transformation. The criteria provide the keystone elements that must be present in the application for consideration:

1. The school library's mission, goals, and objectives relate to the mission, goals, and objectives of the school's and district's long-range plan.
2. The school library is continuously assessed and evaluated to ensure that it meets the needs of all members of the learning community.
3. The school library is a dynamic learning environment that bridges the gap between equitable access and opportunities for all learners.
4. The library scheduling is thoughtfully designed to ensure learners have access to school library services, spaces, and resources at the point of need.

Download a copy of the rubric (ala.org/aasl/awards/nsly) to begin your own self-assessment so that you will have a clearer idea of where you may need to concentrate resources and efforts.

The 2019 NSLY recipient, High School District 214, located in Arlington Heights, Illinois, is a clear example of a district-wide program that uses the AASL Standards as the focal point of its approach to developing a strong brand. In a press release announcing the recipient, Rob Hilliker, chair of the NSLY Award Committee, noted:

> The decisive point for the committee was the depth and richness of the collaboration among the administrators and school librarians. We were also highly impressed by the integration of programming and service delivery with local public libraries, and the rich educational partnerships with local businesses to promote authentic, project-based inquiry learning for their students. (ALA/AASL 2019)

Whereas recipients prior to 2019 were scored with a rubric representing criteria from previous standards, many of the libraries recognized have continued to evolve their brands in alignment with current standards. Fran Glick, then coordinator of library media programs for the 2017 recipient, Baltimore County Public Schools, specifically identified the concept of rebranding as a contributing factor in the school libraries' evolution:

> Over the past several years, the district has made significant strides in rebranding the role of the school librarian. The transformation of teaching and learning toward customized and personalized student learning is equally evident in our school libraries. Our school system's philosophy regarding school libraries—and their place at the heart of student learning—is affirmed by a staffing model which ensures that all schools are staffed by a full-time certified school librarian. (ALA/AASL 2017)

Another strong example of a school librarian who has really embraced the need to ensure that a service culture permeates the codevelopment of the school library is manifested in a *Knowledge Quest* blog post entitled "Co(mmunity)-Constructed Library" by Iris Eichenlaub. Iris is the librarian/technology integrator at Camden Hills Regional High School in Rockport, Maine. She notes in her opening paragraph,

> I'm the steward of the school library. It's my job to make the library a place that reflects our learning community and responds to the community's needs. Since our population of users is always changing, this means the library will also adapt, iterate, and grow in response. When I invite participation from our teachers and students, it means I am committed to manifesting those ideas (to the best of my ability and within reason). (Eichenlaub 2019)

We couldn't have said it better! These are words to live by and indicative of a school librarian who embraces the concept of a service culture and is responsive and alert to the needs of the learning community she serves. Questions posed at the conclusion of Eichenlaub's blog post are included in this chapter's "Questions for the Reflective Practitioner" (questions 4 and 5) because they further illustrate what we believe to be true—she is the Nordstrom of her school because she knows her users and is responsive to their needs. We all need to be the Nordstrom of our schools.

Questions for the Reflective Practitioner

1. What kinds of memories do your library users have about their experiences with your school library?

2. What rules and regulations can you revisit, revise, or eliminate to make the school library more hospitable?

3. How can you commit to the overall school library brand promoted in the AASL Standards and ensure more consistency of user experience?

4. How does your learning community inform your school library practices?

5. Does your community have input into the policies, programs, collection, and physical space in your school library?

School Library Brand versus Personal Brand

Individual commitment to a group effort—that is what makes a team work, a company work, a society work, a civilization work.
—*Vince Lombardi (n.d.)*

Although many practitioners have a personal brand, those who have been able to cultivate the school library brand vis-à-vis a standards-based approach make the longest and most lasting impact on the school culture and the community. It is mindfulness of "we" before "me" that is the raison d'etre of the school library program—to serve all learners, not our personal agendas and interests. Although we all want to bring our talents, strengths, and passions to our situations, we need to first focus on grounding our practice in the AASL Standards. Although there are any number of other education- or technology-related organizations and entities that we may participate in or follow, serious school librarians recognize that AASL and its parent group, ALA, are the voice of the profession because these organizations develop standards through a representative body of qualified members.

Standards-based consistency of experience in your preparation and professional practice is essential because, without it, long-term success and sustainability are at risk. How often have we witnessed the collapse of a school library and its programs when a person leaves their position and their successor goes off in a whole new direction without considering standards and the specific culture and needs of the learning community?

The school library brand is part of the climate and culture we foster in the physical space and digital spaces through library transactions as well as through relationships we develop with stakeholders. Brand is expressed through publications, websites, blogs and comments, tweets, our social media accounts, and all digital traces of online activities. We now realize that a brand is somewhat like a tattoo—easier to create than to remove.

Our Survey and Representative Sample

A brand is also more than a logo or slogan—it is the expectations that others have about you and your school library. To help illustrate and consider the many ways one can go about fostering those expectations, we administered a questionnaire to numerous school library professionals who are either well established in the field or emerging in the area of brand recognition. In identifying who to contact, we ensured that all service levels were included—elementary school, middle school, and high school building-level practitioners, district-level supervisors, and pre-service educators. We were mindful of geographic and population density representation and considered diversity in gender and ethnic/racial identification.

The sample we surveyed is not an exhaustive list of branding powerhouses; however, the survey resulted in a resonant response that helped us identify a spectrum of thoughts about what a school library brand really is.

The Questions, Select Responses, and Common Themes

Although the task was difficult, we edited selected excerpts to best demonstrate how practitioners foster brand development and loyalty. We are delighted to share and ponder some really brilliant thinking from the field.

Describe how you developed your school library brand in relation to your school, its needs, and its culture.

Sue Kowalski: Most stakeholders would connect us with a place that is positive, learner-centered, compassionate, and embedded in all aspects of teaching, community, and culture.

Tracey Wong: Every different school library I have worked in, I have had to adapt to the environment, but one common theme I found was that learners wanted a place they could be themselves, have choices, and have fun.

Jessica Gilcreast: Just watch and listen. Watch for patterns and listen to the questions they ask at the circ desk. These are your cues for making changes to benefit your school. Be a change agent and enjoy the opportunity to reinvent yourself all the time!

Shannon DeSantis Giles: I spent the first year cultivating a sense of belonging. The library was the school's central learning commons: a place where you could walk in the room with a friendly face welcoming you, helping you find the right book, hear booktalks, program robots, learn research skills, troubleshoot technology, or proofread your paper.

COMMON THEMES: BRAND DEVELOPMENT

» Safe space and sense of belonging
» Community engagement/environmental needs
» School curriculum/mission alignment
» School librarian's professional passion area and authenticity

Iris Eichenlaub: This process started with changing and developing the culture of the school library from what was a fairly traditional approach (silent, carpeted, no food or drink, overdue fines, outdated and stagnant collection) to a learner-centered, user input–driven space for community engagement.

Sandy Yamamoto: The school library has supported the school brand of Caring, Dignity, and Integrity (CDI). Inquiry-based lessons encourage personal choice and voice; ethical decision making when using information/technology; and respect for others, the environment, and themselves.

Rebecca Wynkoop: We opened our school four years ago, brand new. I had a year to prepare for the opening, a year to work closely with a design team of administrators and department heads, to build the vision for the library in our school. Once mission and vision were agreed upon, we began to discuss how we were going to build community, not just for the library but for the whole school.

Tom Bober: The school library's brand is focused on four areas—loving and celebrating literature, connecting learners with books, historical thinking, and inquiry. That branding stems from two pillars. First, needs were identified that were not consistently being met by classroom educators and others around those four areas. Second, the school library, meaning the collection, available offerings, and the librarian (me), were able to meet those needs.

Anita Cellucci: The development of the brand began as I shifted my focus to the social and emotional wellness of the school community. . . . At the time, our school was seeing a steep incline of anxiety, depression, and suicidal ideation with our students, and our educators felt helpless.

Kathy Carroll: I met with the principal, asked lots of questions about his vision, and then aligned the school library's brand to his long-range strategic plan. For example, if he wanted more literacy, that is what I focused on providing. I also shared with him my vision for the space and how it was possible to personalize the space, focus on his vision, and still remain aligned with the AASL *National School Library Standards.*

BEHIND THE DESIGN:
UH MANOA LIS PROGRAM LOGO

An unexpected "Easter egg" arrived because of sending our questionnaire to branding pros in the school library field. By coincidence, the Library and Information Science (LIS) program at the University of Hawai'i Manoa (UH Manoa) had recently completed a rebrand of its marketing materials as a faculty-student endeavor. In a February 2021 e-mail interview by Susan D. Ballard, Dr. Violet Harada shared the backstory—a great example of how a community approaches development of a shared message and identity.

In spring 2019, as part of an effort to step up recruiting efforts, the LIS program at UH Manoa decided a new logo would help with a renewed push to market the LIS program to prospective students. After discussions with graphics design Professor Chae Ho Lee, it was decided that a logo redesign would be his senior seminar's semester-long project for spring 2020. This project entailed initial meetings with Lee; several meetings throughout the semester with his students, our students, and faculty for questions and answers about the program and its needs; and two rounds of presentations from the graphic design students. In the end, a committee of two faculty members and two LIS student leaders voted for the final design. The logo by Jana Sasaki was selected for its combination of centering Hawai'i and library resources and focusing on forward momentum for the program. Cheri Ebisu, LIS program coordinator, facilitated the work from start to finish.

Fran Glick: We developed a brand for our school system's libraries, and through professional learning and marketing, encouraged the community of professionals to define their school libraries, programs, and practices via the "brand." Our hashtag (#bcpslms) became a unifier in our work as we demonstrated evidence of who and what we are.

Diana Rendina: My focus is tying our school library brand in with the school mission. I've created hashtags related to recommended books (#terpreads) and makerspace activities (#terpmakers). I frequently promote our school library Instagram account as a way to promote our library brand.

Anatomy of Logo/Brand Development

NAVIGATION

A traditional voyaging canoe with a hull and two sails used to represent teamwork, unity, and progress

SHARED FOUNDATION

The hull of the canoe represents the shared space and equal access the library provides in a community

TECHNOLOGY

The abstracted canoe sails also form triangular play buttons as a reference to contemporary technology

PALM LEAVES

Stylized palm leaves are used to symbolize peace, longevity, and renewal

FORWARD PROGRESS

Angles and curves in the design indicate a right-facing momentum to create a sense of dynamism and progress toward the future

LIBRARY RESOURCES

The overall form of an open book on its side highlights the LIS Program's involvement in librarianship

Sources: Logo design created in 2020 by student Jana Sasaki, under the direction of Dr. Chae Ho Lee in the UH Manoa Graphic Design Program for the UH Manoa Library and Information Science program. "Anatomy of Logo/Brand Development" infographic created by the University of Hawai'i LIS program.

Cicely Lewis: In our current political and social climate, I knew that my students were hurting and needed something different. After coming across the May 2017 "Stay Woke" edition of *Essence* magazine, I founded and launched the Read Woke movement at my school library.

Rebecca Sofferman: [Collaborating], building relationships with teachers, highlighting what I have to offer (both expertise and resources), and developing lessons and activities in the co-teaching model that are relevant and useful to classroom educators.

How do you feel you have helped the school library brand grow?

Sue Kowalski: I'm passionate and am never content.

IdaMae Craddock: I've shown that school libraries are changing. School libraries are at the intersection of ideas and information. Learners and other educators who wander in with a kernel of wondering walk out with the ability, information, materials, and encouragement they need to make their idea real.

Hilda Weisberg: By presenting at conferences, teaching, writing extensively (practical and accessible books and articles), and maintaining a blog. By curating information for school librarians.

Juan Rivera: Facebook, Twitter, Instagram, DonorsChoose grants that also get the school library attention. Active participation in national, state, and local library associations.

Rebecca Sofferman: I've worked hard to get a place for myself at the table when lessons and activities are being planned, which made sure the administrators recognized the necessity of the school library. When it isn't possible to be part of the planning meetings, I reach out to classroom educators individually and offer suggestions related to the curriculum. Sometimes it's even just some fun activities that I think the students will enjoy. The fun stuff brings them in; the expertise keeps them coming back.

Ali Schlipp: I hope that I convey how much I love my job and that [doing so] has not only encouraged others to pursue school librarianship as their profession but [also] to innovate a school library of their own. By sharing my school library story, it has inspired others to make a change or pursue a project or new collaboration.

Fran Glick: Having a defined vision for our school libraries, and contributions at the school and district levels, positioned our libraries as a model that others looked to as an exemplar.

Diana Rendina: I've built a brand—and, I think, a library culture—from scratch. By consistently sharing what we're doing in the school library through Instagram, e-mail, newsletters, the school blog, assembly announcements, [and the like], I've been reinforcing our school library as a space that is welcoming, open to all, and a haven for creativity.

Becky Calzada: As district coordinator, I have helped in the following ways:

- Reminding school librarians of the importance of telling the school library story; this can be through social media, newsletters, reports, videos, [and so on].

- Sharing info about our brand whenever school librarians or I present or share at conferences; our brand speaks to our reputation and the work we do.

- Making sure our brand/vision is posted on all school library websites.

Mary Lou O'Connor: I have worked it like separate puzzle pieces that need to all fit together into one big picture to successfully meet my district, school, and personal professional development goals and plans, and our AASL *National School Library Standards.*

Cicely Lewis: Read Woke has expanded and was incorporated in many school libraries across the world. Using this program, I have been able to share the power of reading with librarians across the world by speaking at several conferences and writing articles for scholarly journals. I believe that this movement has truly shown the world the power of school librarians.

COMMON THEMES: GROWING YOUR BRAND

» Writing research, books, and articles
» Social media
» Presenting at conferences
» Collaboration and involvement in curriculum/planning
» Building community/safe space

How do you manage the school library brand in relation to your personal brand?

Juan Rivera: I cross post. . . . I make sure when the message is personal that it is genuine and that only a small percentage of posts are asking for donations [and the like]. The rest of my posts are about celebrating the community, the learners, and the resources in action.

Barbara Johnson: My personal brand is a Twitter account. My library brand is that the school library is an evolving place where we play, experiment, and create! My school library changes each year with the learners that come through its doors—they bring new ideas, curiosities, and innovations, driving the library to change, grow, and meet their needs.

Diana Rendina: I try to keep the two separate, in part because of my school's social media policies. My school library brand is more focused on book recommendations, maker programs specific to my library, [and so on]. My personal brand is geared toward other educators and librarians and focuses more on reimagining our library spaces and creating vibrant and engaging makerspaces.

Cecily Lewis: I started my nonprofit in order to separate the two brands. I have social media accounts for the school library as well as my personal social media accounts. Sometimes, I cross post, but most of the time I keep them separate.

Tom Bober: I'd say there is some overlap. Much of the work that I share into the world around the use of primary sources or historically based picture books either originates in the school library or finds its way there after being shared more widely under the umbrella of historical thinking, inquiry, or celebrating literature. These two brands are not identical, but they coexist. My desire to share more widely (which helped to create my personal brand) came directly from the work that I initiated in the school library. Over the years, they both have evolved, but they still overlap. And I think it is important to ask: Why are they not the same? Why aren't the school library brand and my personal brand identical? Simply, the needs aren't identical.

COMMON THEMES: BRAND MANAGEMENT

» Separate accounts/cross posting
» Audience/messaging

What competencies/dispositions help to promote the school library brand?

Pam Harland: Building intentional relationships with all stakeholders, clear communication, confidence, bravery (risk-taking), job crafting (the ability to shift your position to reflect more accurately your personal values), and the ability to accept ambiguity and move forward.

Deb Kachel: Persistence, recognizing these are long-term goals, good communication skills, being able to form and lead a team, being positive.

Tracey Wong: Flexibility, no fear of failure or risk-taking, being open minded and always reaching higher even though it might seem crazy at the time.

Susan Grisby: Flexibility, creativity, solid understanding of pedagogy and how school library standards fit into classroom/subject standards, and a willingness to deliver a "yes and" attitude. I think you have to really love the job, and I do.

Shannon DeSantis Giles: Based on the ALA PSELs [Professional Standards for Educational Leaders] competencies, I think that the school library brand touches on all of them! School librarians use social media to tell their story and their library's story. Social media provides the vehicle to give each narrative its own space in the world.

Ann Ewbank: Communication, Collaboration, Consensus.

Iris Eichenlaub: I believe an essential competency/disposition for a school librarian is to feel empowered, to believe that your work in the library—the services we offer, the collaborations with other educators and learners, the relationships, the books and research and lessons and crafts and fun—MATTERS and HAS VALUE to our learning community.

Sandy Yamamoto: Persistence, flexibility, a thick skin, focus.

Rebecca Wynkoop: You really have to love the job. You have to want to be with students. You have to be willing to put yourself "out there" in ways that most educational professionals don't. You have to be willing to work alone and collaboratively all at the same time. The success of an entire school library program rests on the shoulders of one librarian, in most cases. This can be an incredible burden to bear even in a school where the library is supported, funded, and valued. You have to have the ability to continue to press on, even in the face of the interminable misrepresentation or misunderstanding of the work you do.

Ali Schlipp: A genuine love of school librarianship; being an advocate is paramount! Also I think each librarian has a special talent or focus. As an alt-hire to the field, it allowed me to utilize my theater and multimedia degree, and my colleagues who were education majors or public librarians switching to a school setting found that working with me diversified our project skill set.

Anita Cellucci: Reflective practices also help to promote the brand as I believe it's important to be authentic to ourselves and our learners and not to have a brand to promote self.

COMMON THEMES: COMPETENCIES/DISPOSITIONS

» Passion
» Persistence
» Flexibility
» Two-way communication

Do you have any advice on challenges or pitfalls in relation to brand development and management?

Pam Harland: I guess there must be some psychological research about the desire to be famous (name recognition) for humans. I had that desire in my 30s. As I matured, I realized that "fame" (in the world of school librarians!) had nothing to do with what really mattered to me. As I learned to recognize my personal core values, I clearly understood that what was important to me was helping to elevate school librarianship and help future school librarians reach their full potential.

Sue Kowalski: The school library brand message needs to be conveyed in human words, not library terms. It needs to be about lifelong learning, not just grade-level learning. It needs to align with building and district goals and mission, to be flexible to be applied to lots of arenas, to be visionary but not too trendy, and to be "out there" consistently so people know it. Of equal importance is the action and impact the school library is making, so the brand is more than just a phrase or tag line.

IdaMae Craddock: First, build political capital. Do favors. Do things for classroom educators, for colleagues, for administrators, for parents. Make yourself really useful. Your community will have way more patience for controversial decisions if they are partners instead of patrons. Next, have really, really good, well thought out, learner-centered reasons for every decision you make. Whether it's big like genrefying or small like just moving the soft seating from one side to the other. Have good reasons and tell them to people a lot. Finally, walk the walk. If you are about inclusion and access, then you can't develop complicated pass systems or close the school library for inventory. If you are about a robust collection, then you need to be out there on the bookmobile or on a cart. If your school library is about creativity, then you can't restrict supplies. I understand that it's hard and time consuming and sometimes decisions look impractical from the outside, but you have to have actions that line up with the philosophy that you've communicated.

Tracey Wong: My advice is to move into zones of being uncomfortable. That makes you continue to learn and to take risks. By doing so you grow yourself personally and professionally and your brand. If you are not growing, you are not developing and you are stagnant and that is not a good place for your school library or for advocacy.

Heather Moorefield-Lang: Brand development and management can take up a lot of time whether it's social media, websites, or more. It is easy to get something started and find that you lag in the middle of the year when things get busy. Having your brand management, site, and social media maintenance as part of your weekly schedule is important.

Gail Dickinson: You have to believe it personally. It has to be the most important thing that you want to accomplish. It has to be the way that you view the world.

Ann Ewbank: Buy-in takes time.

Sandy Yamamoto: It takes time to figure out a vision and even more time to implement the process and practices in order to reach it.

Rebecca Wynkoop: My advice would be to develop the brand collaboratively. Bring learners, other educators, administrators, and families into the conversation. What do they need? How do the needs of your community inform the brand you are building?

Kathy Carroll: The key is to be very specific and to research the demographics and interests of both your learners and the surrounding community. It must meet their needs and generate interest; otherwise, the best branding in the world will still be ineffective.

Fran Glick: Stay true to your ideal. Tell your story—again and again.

Barbara Johnson: It can be overwhelming! Pick ONE social media platform to get started (I began on Twitter). Take LOTS of pictures—I use them for promotion, for my evaluations, for my end of year reports, for presentations, for training, and for me to remember what we do!

Diana Rendina: Be authentic. Be yourself. Students can tell when someone is trying too hard, and they don't like it.

Becky Calzada: Anyone wanting to capitalize on brand development must understand that the thoughtful investment of time, planning, and consideration of brand development goes a long way, and you move forward. Being clear on the purpose and expectations for use of the brand is also important in guiding others in the use of the brand.

Cecily Lewis: Share your story and don't be afraid to ask for help. Reach out to other organizations doing the same work as you and collaborate. I also highly recommend writing grants and joining a professional learning community.

COMMON THEMES: ADVICE FROM PEERS

- » Resist "fame" and focus on your community and your authentic self.
- » Cultivate partners, not patrons.
- » Communicate, Communicate, Communicate.
- » Back up your brand with actions.
- » Continue to push beyond your comfort zones.
- » It takes time, investment, and strategic planning.

How do you continue to adjust and improve brand experience?

Deb Kachel: It's taken me a long time, but I think I've found my "spot" and purpose. I do make tweaks as I work with other stakeholders and learn their concerns, often embedding their language in mine.

Sue Kowalski: Constantly looking at what we do, what we should do, and what we can do to empower kids, grow the program, and make the world a better place. Big goals, but we are never content.

IdaMae Craddock: We are what our patrons make us. It's our calling to provide the resources that they need to make their ideas real. Ten years ago, what they needed to do was different from what they need now, which will be different from what they need in five years. We need to keep anticipating needs, investing in what's next, and listening carefully not only to the research in our field but also to our community.

Jessica Gilcreast: Spending time with learners, asking questions, getting their input and feedback are all ways that I continue to make change. No two years are ever the same and typically just when I think I have one method down for something, I change it. I have a sticker on my laptop: "Only dead fish go with the flow." A little reminder to keep me on my toes.

Hilda Weisberg: I persist. I keep aware of changes in how leadership is seen and manifested in education and in the business world.

Heather Moorefield-Lang: Environmental scan. What is being used, what is no longer relevant, what needs to stay, [what] needs to go. It is important to continuously cull and also be ready to pull the plug when a resource is no longer relevant.

Sandy Yamamoto: I try to take guidance from learners and other educators. They give me great feedback when I talk to them one on one.

Tracey Wong: I improve brand experience by always seeking new partnerships. It might be the chief business officer, other educators, experts. . . . I will work with anyone to make more creation and passion in the school library. Additionally, do not underestimate the power of praise and appreciation. People want to help. They want to make communities better. When you are grateful and sincere and show appreciation, it comes back tenfold.

Tom Bober: Needs change. Our own professional skill sets and areas of expertise grow and change. The task of identifying needs and offerings isn't just a one-time thing. It is something that is done regularly. From that, long- and short-term plans are made to match those needs and offerings, which will reinforce or evolve the brand over time.

Ali Schlipp: I am always striving to provide the best possible space, resources, and experiences for my learners and school community. My mission or brand changes based on the needs of the learners and progress each year. Also, at the risk of being dorky, I feel compelled to protect and represent the profession that brings me so much joy. This is why I love this job—school libraries are always evolving and providing new opportunities.

Kathy Carroll: I revisit the school library strategic plan every year. I recently began using Instagram more than Twitter when I realized that platform was used more frequently by our learners. I even had a couple of TikTok posts created by learners from our Student Advisory Group. Ultimately, I think it is important to stay current with student interest while staying mindful of my goals for the school library and the school's mission.

Barbara Johnson: Constant change! You have to be evolving, we are NEVER doing the same activity, the same way, over again. We evaluate, get feedback, reflect, and relaunch. We are always asking our patrons what we can do to help, improve, and engage them.

Becky Calzada: Stay open to learning about using a brand; this isn't a concept just used in school libraries. I continue to learn about branding from anyone that has a strong brand recognition. Using those known brands as mentors will inspire new ideas for use in your brand development.

COMMON THEMES: CONTINUAL IMPROVEMENT

- » Listen to community/stakeholders/educational landscape.
- » Experiment, experiment.
- » Seek new partnerships.
- » Reevaluate often.
- » Always be a learner.

Questions for the Reflective Practitioner

1. Consider the responses in this chapter to the questionnaire administered. Think about how you would respond to similar questions.

2. Describe how you might develop your school library brand in relation to your school community, its needs, and its culture.

3. How would your approach help the school library brand grow?

4. What kinds of results would you anticipate from your work?

5. How might you manage the school library's brand in relation to your personal brand?

6. Which competencies/dispositions will help you promote the school library brand? Which will you need to further develop?

7. Do you anticipate any challenges or pitfalls in relation to brand development and management? How might you work to mitigate those challenges?

8. How will you continue to adjust and improve brand experience for your community?

Observation, Data, and Action

5

Lasting change is a series of compromises. And compromise is all right, as long [as] your values don't change.
—*Jane Goodall (2002)*

We begin this chapter with words of wisdom from Jane Goodall. However, another remarkable observer, Margaret Mead, also said, "I learned to observe the world around me, and to note what I saw" (1972). Each woman studied a particular group to the nth degree and knew each and every member as an individual as well as what made them tick. Margaret Mead studied the peoples of Oceania. Her findings were particularly enlightening regarding adolescent development. Goodall's work with the chimpanzees of Gambia was likewise compelling and helped us recognize that societies and norms exist beyond the human experience. Can we say that we have that same understanding about the communities we serve? Are the programs we provide genuinely developed to meet local needs and priorities—or do we create them based on our own preferences?

In the *Chronicle of Higher Education* article "An Anthropologist in the Library," Scott Carlson (2007) shared lessons learned about observation by the University of Rochester after the university hired an anthropologist

> to study undergraduates, to help shed light on how they do their research and write papers, and how they spend their days. The results of the study . . . helped guide a library renovation, influenced a Web-site redesign, led to changes in the way the library markets itself to students, and, in some cases, completely changed the image of undergraduates in the eyes of Rochester librarians. (Carlson 2007, A26)

Although the anthropologist hired, Nancy Fried Foster, had been involved in more traditional forms of study, there was no need to set up a "blind" and conduct observation from a neutral vantage point. Rather, the study was approached as "applied" anthropology—the process of taking the methods of anthropology and using them in consumer studies and product design, among other areas. "If you have been making a bunch of assumptions based on out-of-date information," said Foster, "maybe it's time to ask some people some questions." In the instance of the University of Rochester, students and faculty were aware of the observational methods being used and were also active participants in the collection of data and information that would help address how *they* wanted to use the library.

School librarians may not have the funding to hire an anthropologist to assess our learning communities, but, as school librarian Jessica Gilcreast suggested in chapter 4, we can "just watch and listen. Watch for patterns and listen to the questions they ask at the circ desk. These are your cues for making changes to benefit your school. Be a change agent and enjoy the opportunity to reinvent yourself all the time!" Gilcreast further stated that based on her observations, the data told her to

> move furniture and improve traffic flow, weed the collection and genrefy (nobody could find anything!), rebuild the website, remove many of the rules, create better signage and face books *out* (who wants to look at a skinny spine? Show me the full Monty!), add resources that students want (you bet I have a chocolate fountain for checkout!). (Gilcreast, survey response to authors, 2021)

Gilcreast clearly focused development and change on what her clientele told her through their interactions with the school library and what additional data revealed. We all need to embrace the power of observation, and we also need to be willing to take a long, hard look at our practice—warts and all.

To that end, here is a brief retelling of a sad episode in librarianship—one so apparently upsetting to the "powers that be" (or were) that it is hard to find mention of it in contemporary library literature or discussion of it in pre-service education. It is a bit reminiscent of the ancient Roman practice of *damnatio memoriae*, or erasing something from history because we don't like it or because it has been an embarrassment. This story began as a well-intended effort by students and faculty at the University of Maryland (UMD) to provide library services to an underserved, minority community. Thankfully, in 2020 the UMD iSchool website published a piece written by Hayleigh Moore entitled *The High John Library (1967): Shaping the Future of Libraries as Community Resource Centers*, providing some insight into what transpired. The article highlights the controversy that UMD encountered when it challenged the status quo. In the 1960s UMD launched an early diversity initiative by developing a library in Fairmount Heights, Maryland, an economically deprived, predominantly Black community with "limited educational and cultural resources available to its residents." The High John Library (named after an African American folk hero) was created to address community needs and to serve as a lab school for MLS students. As noted by Moore, "for MLS students, the library was the ultimate field study experience, while the college's faculty used the library as a chance to try out new ways to make library services relevant in an urban community that was suffering from wealth disparity and a dearth of resources." Eventually the High John became part of the Prince Georges County Library System; however, as noted by Moore, along the way it encountered a great deal of criticism from the library establishment "for overstepping the established boundaries of the library profession." Critics did not like the fact that the program was centered on a community-driven mission, nor did they condone the goal of specifically educating MLS students about the needs of underserved populations. Ultimately the controversy evolved into organized protest within ALA and led to the creation of the Social Responsibilities Round Table (SRRT), which "still exists today to promote social responsibility as a core value of librarianship and to bring greater field-wide attention to issues of equity, diversity, and inclusion."

With the perspective of time, UMD has been vindicated and its approach to community librarianship validated as more and more libraries understand that they need to be reflective and representative of the community they serve. And, though the High John project provided the genesis of ALA's SRRT and more focus on issues of social justice, some of the criticism leveled at the time came from within the project itself. Richard Moses, an Enoch Pratt Library staffer who was charged with oversight for the student field experience at the branch, indicated in an article for the *ALA Bulletin* that High John was always more about the library students' experience than the community they purported to serve (Yamauchi, 2018). Such criticism makes the point of view of James Welbourne all the more poignant. Welbourne was hired as a UMD faculty member post–High John and was specifically charged to recruit and train students of color because part of the failure of the initial project was that "all of the initial twelve students were White (eleven were women), and once on the ground 'were clearly suffering from cultural shock' in the poor Black community."

> We must turn the effective practice and control of libraries over to people who are competent and capable of doing it and, in the process, throw away all those rigid controls which have kept the profession irrelevant. Those controls have only let in people who cannot do the job and kept out the most capable people. And that is hard for people to face, that they themselves are irrelevant, they themselves are the problem. If they would only get out of the way, the people could solve their own problems. If people in the inner city had the resources that one uses to go about problem solving, some of these critical problems could be solved. (Welbourne, 1972, 109)

School Library Data

What can school librarians learn from experiments such as the High John when there are still library purists who insist that a library and librarian must conform to a mold that is no longer relevant? School librarians need to recognize that services must be demand-driven and grounded in learning community needs, not our preconceived notions and biases about those needs. School librarian Iris Eichenlaub used her powers of observation and her knowledge of her users to conclude:

> So the brand . . . is a student-centered library. The library is a hub of our school community, a safe place, a fun and relaxing place, a place to take time out for a break, or a place to study alone or with friends, a place to make connections with caring adults (that's us, library staff!), a place to find a listening ear or to get help with a project, or to find supplies (notecard or scissors, glue stick, pen, or a condom from the condom bowl), a place to "see" yourself represented in our collection or our displays (which extends into our digital collections and social media presence), a safe place where you feel affirmed in your identities. (Eichenlaub, survey response to authors, 2021)

When thinking about "demand-driven practice," in addition to using observation, we are also empowered by using data to inform our work and to develop action plans. Most school librarians are familiar with library-specific data sources, but let's review to ensure that we are making the most of them.

Access Data

This type of data deals with physical and intellectual access to the facilities, resources, and services that school libraries provide. Such data consider

- days/hours open and closed and for what purpose (testing, etc.),
- schedule (fixed, flexible, or responsive combination),
- organization of resources (Dewey Decimal Classification system, genre, or combination), and
- resources accessible per Americans with Disabilities Act (ADA) standards.

Physical Space Data

When considering physical space data, the emphasis is on whether the space can

- accommodate one class for instruction,
- accommodate individuals and small groups working independently,
- be ADA compliant,
- accommodate the collection, furnishings, and equipment,
- be flexible, allowing for different configurations depending upon need, and
- house a production or innovation area.

Staffing Data

In using staffing data, the focus is on the qualifications and number of staff to provide service to a learning community. Staffing data include the following classifications:

- Credentialed—holding a state endorsement as a school librarian
- Alternative certification—state-issued letter of eligibility as a school librarian
- Credentialed teacher—holding a state teaching credential with no school librarian endorsement and being paid as a teacher
- Classified employee—paraprofessional, aide, clerk, technician, assistant, and the like, not paid as a teacher
- Hours worked/paid—more than full-time; full-time; half-time; less than half-time
- Extended year days for staff, beyond those required by contractual agreement
- Adult volunteer(s) and hours worked

Resources Data

In the area of data related to resources, school librarians examine the technologies/resources available in or through the school library:

- Physical number of books or other content formats
- Print and electronic subscriptions to magazines, journals, and newspapers
- Automated catalog
- Library web page *with* access to online library catalog
- Library web page *without* access to online library catalog
- Automated library circulation
- Automated textbook circulation
- Wireless Internet access for learners
- Collaboration software (e.g., SharePoint, Google Drive)
- Paid online access to full-text periodicals, full-text reference books, primary sources, or other subscription databases or portals in the school library
- Remote access to paid online full-text periodicals, full-text reference books, primary sources, or other subscription databases or portals
- DVDs/video collection, video streaming, or both
- Audio books (in any format—e.g., for MP3 player, Playaways)
- E-book readers/portable devices
- Integrated online information searching that includes your library catalog, paid-access databases, and open educational resources
- Computers housed and available in the school library for direct instruction and student use
- Devices available for sign-out (computers, tablets) and hotspots

Collaboration, Social Networking, and Communication Data

This area of data collection considers whether required Children's Internet Protection Act (CIPA) filtering software allows for access to web-based productivity and collaboration tools (e.g., wikis, blogs, online document editors, or similar tools) via the school network and what types of tools are used and how:

- Online publishing (e.g., blogs, including a library-based blog)
- Photo- and video-sharing sites (e.g., Flickr, Google Photo, Vimeo, Shutterfly)
- Photo- and video-sharing social networks (e.g., Twitter, Instagram, Facebook, TikTok)
- RSS and news feeds (e.g., CNN, NYT)
- Image generators (e.g., Animoto, Pixton)
- Tagging and social bookmarks (e.g., Pinterest, Wakelet, Padlet)
- Wikis (e.g., PBworks, MediaWiki)
- Online productivity tools (e.g., Google Docs, Open Office, Canva)
- Cloud-based file hosting (e.g., Dropbox, Box.com)
- Social library (e.g., LibraryThing, Goodreads)
- Video (e.g., YouTube, TeacherTube, SchoolTube, Hulu)
- Downloadable audio files (e.g., podcasts)
- E-books and audiobooks (e.g., Sora, OverDrive)
- Virtual school/course/classroom (e.g., Blackboard, Moodle, Schoology)
- Videoconferencing (e.g., Skype, GoTo Meeting, Zoom, Google Meet)
- Student e-mail accounts
- A library social media account (e.g., Twitter, Facebook)

Usage Data

Who uses the facilities, collections, and services that school libraries provide and for what purposes? Usage data collection will help you answer these questions. Include such categories as these:

- Circulation records (monthly and average daily)
- Collection maps
- Number of classes scheduled
- Individual use including before, during, and after school
- Units of study supported by grade/subject area and level of collaboration (figure 5.1)

School:			Month:		Year:				
Project/ Research Topic	No. of Sections	Grade Level / Subject Area	No. of Days	No. of Classes	Level of Collaboration				
					1	2	3	4	5

LEVELS OF COLLABORATION

1. No collaboration beyond scheduling the school library and offering assistance to classroom educators and learners.
2. Schedule the school library and curate resources for use in the library, in the classroom, or remotely.
3. Introduce resources at the beginning of the unit as well as curate resources and schedule.
4. Plan with classroom educators, offering suggestions and strategies as well as instruction, scheduling, and resource gathering.
5. Provide a lesson in information literacy or concept as a result of planning with classroom educators, as well as instruction, scheduling, and resource gathering.

FIGURE 5.1

Level of collaboration rubric

Budget Data

An analysis of the budget that supports the school librarian's work considers several financial factors:

- Funds allocated for the purchase of books—both print and digital titles (e-books)—and processing costs if purchased with books
- Funds allocated for the purchase of school library materials other than books
  - Periodicals (paper or electronic)
  - Technology and media resources and related equipment

- Funds available for supplies, equipment, and furnishings (replacement and new)
- Funds available for conferences and professional development
- Sources of funding to purchase library materials
  - General (district or school)
  - Fund-raising (e.g., parent groups, book fairs, DonorsChoose)
  - Title I (or other federal sources)
  - Donations
  - Other (e.g., one-time discretionary grants to the school/district)

Community Data

Although standard means of assessing libraries are useful, there are yet other indicators and means of observation that can help school librarians elevate demand-driven practice. From the perspective of the AASL Standards personas, or personas you have created, think about the members of your learning community. Do you know what motivates them? Or are they puzzles to you? What are the intrinsic values of the community—what are your community members proud of, and what is the basic community culture as evidenced by their shared beliefs, customs, and behaviors? How is the community organized? How are communications handled? How does the community deal with mistakes or deviation, approach problems, and honor and ritualize people or events, and how does it accept new members? Consider various scenarios for working with and for the personas you adopted or created. By doing so, and by becoming familiar with and thoroughly mining the following data, you will be able to develop an accurate profile of your community.

Demographic Data

Understanding and using local demographics are essential for improving our work. Include the following elements in your data collection:

- Community history
- Geographic location
- Population (racial/ethnic composition; religious affiliations)
- Size of average household and percentage of school-age population
- Employment status and educational background
- Housing composition and trends
- Crime rate
- Economic base

Student Data

Use of student data assists in creating a profile (dare we say "persona") that provides school librarians a more complete picture of who we are serving, and the following elements are useful indicators:

- Enrollment
- Attendance
- Drop-out and graduation rate
- Parent income, education, and employment
- Free and reduced-price lunch rates
- Discipline indicators

School Data

School librarians need to know specifics that help define needs and improve our services:

- History
- Funding mechanisms
- Physical plant
- Number of classroom educators, administrators, support staff
- Educational background and experience of staff
- Learner-educator ratios
- Library and technology statistics
- Special programs

School District Data

As with school-level data, it is helpful to be aware of and use district-wide information:

- History
- Governance
- Organizational structure
- Funding mechanism
- Special programs and services provided

Perceptions Data

All the aforementioned data sources allow school librarians to get a snapshot or baseline impression of instructional and program needs, utilization, and effectiveness. But the most compelling use of these data is in combination with "perceptions data," which reveal the learning community's satisfaction or dissatisfaction with the school library brand. In addition to ongoing observation of how people engage (or do not engage) with the brand, other methods will further develop this information and create a continuous feedback loop to help us understand what learners, parents, other educators, administrators, staff, and the community think about the school library brand. This effort ensures that we are focused on improvement through an ongoing process of collecting data about the user experience, analyzing these data, and then using the results to implement interventions or changes that we then can assess to determine effectiveness. In the digital age, school librarians should take a cue from the business world by automating data collection. We can use online instruments (such as SurveyMonkey or Google Forms) to create questionnaires/surveys as well as e-mail and text messages that include a feedback link to rate a service or experience. Word-processed interviews, focus group transcripts, and observation/field notes can be searched for key words, patterns, and trends that will illuminate the process.

- Questionnaires/surveys
- E-mail and text messages
- Interviews
- Focus groups
- Observation/field notes

Additional Data Sources

Other data collection sources to consider include grades and test scores, checklists/ charts, photographs, journal entries, rubrics, and student products/projects and portfolios.

Translating Observations and Data into Action

We have now returned full circle to the work of Jane Goodall and Margaret Mead. Again, they were faithful and patient observers of the groups they studied, collecting data and evidence that helped them understand and articulate what they discovered and learned about their subjects. This is also our challenge in developing the school library brand—to consider what the evidence is telling us, to devise appropriate strategies to address needs, and to act accordingly. Although it is great to also have a personal brand and to participate in activities designed to develop and expand our professional competencies, unless these activities are aligned with the specific needs of our learning communities, there is cause for reflection. Without this reflection, we risk being more concerned about our own personal "brands" and how many followers, likes, or "mentions" we get. In addition, we should be discerning about professional development. Its focus must be on promoting the interests of learners and improving the school library rather than on promoting ourselves.

STAYING GROUNDED: TWO PERSPECTIVES

"I think early in my career I tried too hard to be taken seriously on a bigger stage instead of focusing intently on my school, my learners, and my library. In this day and age of easy accessibility to social media, I think it can be quite easy to get caught up in branding and oversharing. Now that I've been doing this a while, I am quite content to be doing the best I can do right here in my own school library whether anyone else in library land knows about it or not. That's not to say I'm done presenting at conferences or sharing my ideas—just to say that's not at the top of my agenda."

—Susan Grigsby (school librarian, Tokyo, Japan)

"Don't be afraid to modify your brand but try to land on one that resonates with you and those you hope will follow and join you. If your brand is developed for the good of K–12 learners and their needs (not yourself or maintaining jobs for school librarians), then no one can challenge your brand."

—Deb Kachel (school library educator, Antioch University)

Data-Inspired Questions, Data-Driven Responses

We have adapted David Brier's *How to Rebrand: 19 Questions to Ask Before You Start* (2015) to create a list of five questions for you to consider in developing the brand for *your* community. Use these questions as a lens through which to view your school library and your learning community, the data you have, and the data you can collect to inform your actions.

Why are we doing a rebrand—a brand rehab, an update, or is there a specific problem we need to resolve?

Be mindful that there must be a reason—don't fall into the trap of rebranding for rebranding's sake. You want to lead with brand direction, not just follow a trend. Are we doing something because everyone else is or because we are susceptible to the "initiative du jour" syndrome? Make sure that you have an objective *based on the evidence* that something needs to be fixed, changed, or modified. If it works, don't "fix" it.

Has there been a change in the landscape that is impacting our growth potential?

We live in a world in which change and disruption are rapid and pervasive. School librarians need to be nimble and responsive when the landscape shifts. If you have never seen the Merrie Melodies cartoon "Duck Amuck" featuring Daffy Duck endlessly tormented by an offscreen animator (revealed at the end) who keeps changing the scene, thus requiring Daffy to shift gears continuously all the while becoming more and more aggravated, it's worth tracking down for a laugh (youtube.com/watch?v=6X vXsuSJ-1A). But the point is that, in fact, Daffy's predicament is pretty similar to what school librarians must deal with—change is inevitable, and we need to focus not only on the ways in which economic, cultural, and societal changes will impact the work we do but also on using *data and evidence to be strategic* about our response.

Has our customer profile changed?

The school library brand should assure the stakeholders and target group(s) that their agenda(s) will be assisted and amplified by what the school librarian and library have to offer. How do you identify these stakeholders and target groups? What do you know about them, about their priorities and interests? What do you need to find out? Whom do you know who might have the information you need? What research might you need to do? As you seek answers to these questions, a continuous data feedback loop pays dividends. Additionally, automating your data collection methods helps achieve a greater understanding of who your customers are and how their needs have evolved.

Are we pigeonholed as something that we (and our customers) have outgrown?

Are we relevant to the members of our learning community? Do they recognize our purpose? Do we convey a sense of who we are and what we do as well as when and where we do it and for whom? Think about the UMD High John story discussed in this chapter. How can school librarians and libraries be more responsive to community needs? What sorts of *data and evidence will assist us to redefine ourselves effectively and efficiently* in a way that personalizes experiences with the school library and creates meaning and identity?

Is the goal of this rebrand a stepping-stone (evolutionary) or a milestone (revolutionary)?

Are we perceived as progressive and innovative in meeting needs? Are we authentic in developing transparency, cultural context, diversity, and inclusivity? Has a needs assessment helped define short- and long-term goals and objectives? Have you done sufficient *data collection and analysis in order to understand trends and to predict and plan* for when and how to address them?

Questions for the Reflective Practitioner

1. What are some strategies that you might employ in observing how school library users interact with the physical space of the school library?

2. What demographics data will best assist you in developing a profile of your learning community and its needs?

3. How might you go about using focus groups, interviews, or surveys to find out who is not using the school library and why?

4. How do data and evidence inform your professional development needs?

Identifying and Overcoming Barriers

Between the idea / And the reality / Between the motion / And the act /
Falls the Shadow

—*T. S. Eliot (1925)*

S chool librarians often have brand barriers thrown in front of us—and we also often create them ourselves. These barriers must be torn down to have a sustainable brand. The feelings and impressions that members of your school community have when they think of your library, and their memories of the last interaction—positive or negative—are your school library's brand. What you say, your actions, how users interact with your facilities and policies, the perceptions of your culture are your school library brand. Approach the barriers explored in this chapter as opportunities for brand growth and you will also begin to see **brand perception** progress in your learning community of advocates and allies.

Circulation Policies

Policies and procedures are part of the ground rules of the school library and affect the outward face of the library and its brand. School librarians often hear that we are the stewards of the library collection and that we must teach learners responsibility. Yet, if we are asked about the most important part of our job, the predominant response is to increase student literacy. We accomplish this goal by providing access to carefully curated resources in all formats to meet curricular and pleasure reading needs. Policies or rules about lost books and overdue fines or limiting the number of items and length of time items can be signed out work directly against that priority—increasing literacy for learners—and thus against the school library brand.

In a *Knowledge Quest* blog post, Dr. Steve Tetreault (2019) addressed our tendency to adhere to strict circulation policies: "When we let the cost of a book come between a student and their ability to read, we are directly contradicting the purpose of being in education." Tetreault included an anecdote about school librarian Cecily Lewis, who noticed a ninth grader engaged by a book she was reading in the library. Lewis offered to check the book out for her. The learner explained that she'd lost a book in kindergarten and could no longer check out books. When the girl tried to take out books in middle school, she was denied because of the loss of that book years before. The girl was overjoyed when Lewis checked out her books and assured her that she could do so from then on, regardless of previous losses or fines. Lewis's school library brand does not have a circulation barrier. It's welcoming.

Selection Policies

Having the trust of your administration, other educators, and, most importantly, your learners is critically important to brand strength. Establishing trust will also encourage you when it comes to building and maintaining a collection of resources that meet community needs for supporting the curriculum, investigating personal interests, and developing lifelong readers. An inclusive brand ensures that learners will see themselves in the books they read. To fully support learners' explorations of their physical and emotional development, those books must be available at all reading levels and in all genres. As those collection characteristics build, the need for school librarians to have the courage to do the right thing gets clearer. And in the face of challenges, doing the right thing takes a lot of courage. And preparation.

School librarians are facing increased scrutiny as organized groups and well-meaning people seek to protect learners from exposure to ideas that do not reflect their own beliefs. School librarians must be solid in their professionalism, know their responsibilities and rights, and be collaborative with their districts to prepare for the challenges, hopefully before they happen.

Does your school community perceive you as a defender of intellectual freedom? Does your selection policy describe having a collection of materials carefully chosen to be broad and deep? You can break through the barrier of your personal fears, develop needed courage, and have the trust of faculty, administration, and learners when you involve the learning community in your selection process and then face intellectual freedom challenges as a team. Your professionalism, your policy preparation, and your transparency will reinforce trust in your brand.

FROM "FIVE THINGS YOU CAN DO TO SUPPORT INTELLECTUAL FREEDOM IN YOUR LIBRARY"

» Create a culture that supports intellectual freedom by regularly talking about it with users, coworkers, employees, administrators, legislators, and governing bodies.
» Don't wait for a crisis to educate them about the library profession's principles.
» Meet with other organizations and individuals in your community and form partnerships around common interests.

Source: ALA 2021, p. v.

Website

It is indeed a barrier to a welcoming brand if you do not have an easy-to-find, user-friendly, responsive school library website that is as prominent as your school library's front door. First impressions matter, and you need to make a good one. Never mind design or content—does anybody know you are there? When a visitor comes to the district website or school landing page, is there anything immediately accessible about the library? Or is the school library buried several pages in, or, even worse, is the site's search tool required to find it? If the school library is not visible on the website, that obscurity is a result of benign neglect, either by the webmaster or by the school librarian. The often-cited web design axiom "three clicks to find information" is a test of a viable web page. Does it take three clicks or less to reach the school library web page from the district's site? Too often it is hard to know that a school library exists.

Accessibility

As you look at your school library's online presence through a branding lens, consider whether your school community finds an exciting and useful portal to resources. When thinking about accessibility and function, first ask yourself, "Who is this website for?" Look at the personas you created in chapter 2 to begin your redesign and optimize your website for your brand. These audiences are important as you design or redesign your online presence, as indicated in the findings of a study that examined the basic design layout, content, and usability of three hundred randomly sampled school library websites representing all fifty U.S. states (figure 6.1 on the following page).

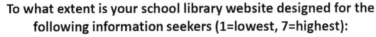

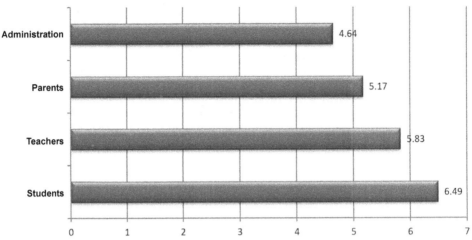

To what extent is your school library website designed for the following information seekers (1=lowest, 7=highest):

- Administration — 4.64
- Parents — 5.17
- Teachers — 5.83
- Students — 6.49

FIGURE 6.1

Who are school library websites designed for?

Source: Chow et al., 2016.

First, evaluate the school library website for usability by learners. Your website must be tailored to learners' interests and their cognitive development. Those two factors are instrumental to school librarians every day in their face-to-face interactions with learners and must be incorporated into your "virtual door" (Valenza 2022) for learners and the community. Second, your site must be easy for learners to navigate. Learners need to be able to find books that they need for schoolwork, personal inquiry, or all-important pleasure reading.

List your staff's names and even pictures as welcoming connections. If you don't include your school e-mail address, please include a library contact e-mail address, the mailing or physical address, and phone number. How can you reach outward and be inclusive for your community or convey accessibility if you are anonymous? Visibility enhances your brand.

Interactions

Users' interactions with the school library, whether in person or virtually, have a significant impact on their perception of the library and their expectations of its brand.

Can your learners put a book on hold remotely? Are their cultures visible, celebrated, and respected on the website? Can they search the website and resources in more than one language? The COVID-19 pandemic made it obligatory for learners to be able to download and enjoy e-books with easy-to-follow directions and a "contact me" link to get help with technology issues directly from you, their school librarian.

Your learners—and their parents—need access to resources for research projects through the school library website, including information, digital, and media literacy tips to locate, evaluate, and cite sources. Collaborating with classroom educators to curate resource lists for projects also strengthens the school library brand immensely and drives up the user statistics, getting the attention of IT staff in your school, and perhaps even resulting in fewer clicks to reach the site.

In his *Knowledge Quest* blog post, "(Re)Building a School Library, Part 1: The Website," Dr. Steve Tetreault (2022) made the connection between rebranding a library and creating a website that places focus on what is happening in that library—the interactions with users. For his middle school library website, Tetreault found that he needed to focus on books and reading, research, media and information literacy, and a calming space.

FIVE THINGS EVERY SCHOOL LIBRARY WEBSITE MUST HAVE

» A focus on teaching
» Examples of student work
» Opportunities for participation
» Evolving resources for your evolving audience
» Flavor

Source: Adapted from LaGarde 2011.

Graphic Design

Given contemporary graphics programs and copyright-free photos, it's not difficult for school library websites to have visual appeal and representation for all learners. Younger learners respond best to big, colorful icons and buttons, whereas high school learners need the website to provide immediate access to high-quality information in all formats. Your library website should reflect and share the vibrancy of your school library and its learning community as you build your brand physically and virtually.

Facility

The use of observation, data, and evidence to inform decision making about your school library facilities can help you see if your brand reflects the behavior that is needed by your learning community. What indicators are there regarding the school library facility that either diminish or elevate the brand experience for someone? Is this a place where learners and educators want to be? Think about how you respond when you are interacting with a particular space or place. What physical, intellectual, and time barriers need to be addressed? Let the AASL Standards be your guide as you work to overcome brand barriers in your school library facility. Focus on aligning your school or district goals and objectives with your school library vision and mission, rather than ending up with a cookie-cutter version of what someone else thinks a school library should be.

User Experience

One of the best quality control checkpoints for any brand and its facilities is to place yourself in the shoes of your customer—simulate their experience for yourself to understand exactly what they will encounter during an interaction with your brand. This is why homeowners are advised to spend a night in their guest room or try sleeping on the pull-out couch, futon, or air mattress they have provided for visitors. You don't want someone searching in the middle of the night for a place to charge their phone when you could easily provide an extension cord from the outlet behind the bed. Or worse yet, have a guest end up at the chiropractor—that is, unless you are hoping that they never visit again! The same practice holds true for the school library. We want everyone to consider the school library the greatest place in the school. We don't ever want to hear that they'll never be back because we provided an unaccommodating environment. We need to look at the space through the lens of our users and consider key elements that are factors in their facility experience.

Signage

The primary purpose of signage is to help direct and inform visitors to a space, but it can also be used to indicate empathy and understanding of the end user experience. As Daniel Pink noted in his book *A Whole New Mind* (2006), we make conscious choices when we decide on the specific message to include in signage. In a blog post on emotionally intelligent signage, Pink (2012) further urged us to consider designing signs that are more likely to produce a desired behavior because they express empathy with the viewer or elicit empathy in the viewer. For example, often the school library limits food or beverages in the facility. So instead of "No eating or drinking," signage with messaging like this may be more effective: "The library is a no food zone, but you are welcome to have water except around computer stations and other electronics for your health and safety, and that of others." Whatever policy you are trying to communicate, do strive to make your signage empathetic. Look at all the messaging about your brand that is done using signage and start taking steps to ensure that it is reflective of the brand loyalty you want to cultivate.

Library Layout

In her book *Library Spaces for 21st-Century Learners* (2013), Margaret L. Sullivan indicated that although we know that library space and furnishings need to be flexible and ADA compliant, an effective way to reimagine the space is to identify zones and create a facility footprint. Such zones would include areas for the collection and technology as well as a variety of seating, workspace, and sound options. Sullivan provided school library scenarios and concepts with relational maps that illustrate this method (pp. 57–66).

Additionally, in *High Impact School Library Spaces* (2015), Sullivan explained that it is vital to understand how people relate with the space and advised use of the AEIOU process (activities, environment, interactions, objects, users) developed by Conifer Research. This process focuses on how people work, what environments they are drawn to, and how they interact in those environments (p. 35). Sullivan also noted that areas such as quiet and collaborative zones need to be branded (p. 68). Not only does this branding help assure users that there is something for everyone, but it also presents an opportunity to promote the message through effective signage, such as the example in figure 6.2 on the following page.

Intellectual Access

How the school library collection is organized communicates something about your brand as well. Is it Dewey, genre, or a mix, and for whose benefit? Are physical resources arranged in a way that is appealing, that merchandises and markets the collection, or is there a reason to maintain a more traditional library look? Has a standard system and nomenclature been adopted throughout a school district or campus to ensure discoverability and a fluid transition from one school level to another, or is this system left to individual or school preferences? Are the needs of non-native English speakers and readers and those who are differently abled considered in the mix? All these factors reflect brand behavior.

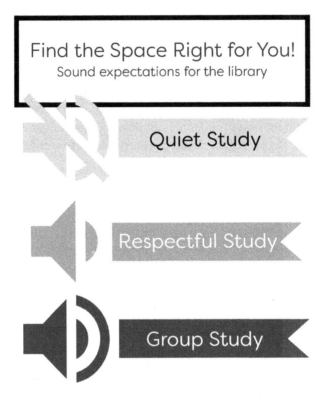

FIGURE 6.2
Find the right space for you

Source: Designed by Erin McCoy (2018), librarian, Massasoit Community College.

Scheduling

Facility access can also be impeded by the use of the space for nonlibrary purposes, such as testing, school pictures, study hall, or detention. Barriers to access and implications for your school library brand can also be set up through schedules that are designed solely as teacher preparation coverage or that are limited to formal classes and instruction without accounting for individual use and needs. AASL's *Position Statement on School Library Scheduling* (2019b) clearly identifies those elements that must be addressed to remove scheduling barriers and improve facility access by all.

Marginalization

Sometimes it may seem as though the school library exists only at the outer edge of the school or appears to be the victim of benign neglect. This type of disregard may manifest in being ignored by the powers that be or in our own indifference to situations or items that need attention. A school librarian may feel isolated because of grade-level or department structures that do not provide representation, much less any input into school priorities, needs, and culture. Such sidelining may be due to the lack of understanding of the role of the school librarian, the residual effect of previous negative experiences that linger with stakeholders, or simply a want of two-way communication that impacts visibility. Let's tackle each of these causes separately to address how to overcome them and build your brand.

Lack of Understanding of the Role

It's important to remember that as brand ambassadors and educators, we are consistently engaged in educating our communities—especially those that start off not understanding that we are indeed educators! School librarians need to emphasize their roles as teacher and instructional partner (AASL 2018b, 14–15) in addition to providing opportunities for self-directed, informal, and formal instruction.

If a classroom educator or principal has never viewed the school library as an integral element in developing the educational experience, it is imperative to demonstrate the value that school librarians bring to the table. Because seeing is believing, and because good news spreads, savvy school librarians will seek out and collaborate with respected classroom educators who want to improve their practice and address learners' academic needs. These educator partners have influence and will help raise our credibility and educate the rest of the faculty and administration about our worth. If resistance is still encountered, then it's worthwhile to appeal to their inner FOMO (fear of missing out) because most educators want to ensure that learners have every chance to succeed, and the school library is where educational opportunity thrives!

Helpful Position Statements

AASL provides position statements (ala.org/aasl/advocacy/resources/statements) aimed at improving understanding of school library efficacy by summarizing the role and purpose of the school library and librarian. Read and internalize the statements' messages, which can serve as talking points while building your brand with stakeholders:

> » *Instructional Role of the School Librarian* (2020)
> » *Role of the School Library* (2019c)
> » *Definition of an Effective School Library* (2018a)

Likewise, activate your own inner FOMO. To educate others about the school library brand, it is important to be present and to become involved in the life of the school and community. Don't isolate yourself. Volunteer to serve on committees, participate in school organizations, and assist with school events where you can connect on a different level with your fellow educators, learners, and parents.

Residual Effect of Previous Negative Experiences

At times it may seem that you are dealing with legacy impressions left by the ghosts of school librarians past, or you yourself may have contributed to a situation that now requires some fence-mending. Whatever the case, set aside your personal feelings and get busy with rebranding! A great place to start is by examining policies and procedures that may be in place to make your life easier but that are onerous to everyone else. You can move from marginalized to celebrated when you make others' lives easier with intention—talk about being memorable! Do you remember the phrase we emphasized in chapter 1? *Every encounter and transaction must support brand expectations.* Not only must you want to, but you need to take advantage of every opportunity to create a positive memory if you are to overcome any lingering doubts about the worth of the school library.

Lack of Two-Way Communication

Communication involves sharing messaging and regular updates on program impact via reports, displays, newsletters, e-mail, press releases, podcasts, a dynamic web presence, social media, and the like and helps engage stakeholders and build brand credibility. Communication also involves providing ongoing opportunities for stakeholders to provide input and assess their own experiences and is equally vital to growing the school library brand. Effective two-way communication helps raise awareness of and commitment to the ongoing success of the school library and lays the groundwork for the development of a financial plan to ensure that success. Too often school librarians are strapped for time and may not complete the communication loop with stakeholders. User engagement is essential for effective communication. Learning communities involved in conversations about the school library are more likely to be aware of and invested in its brand, so make time for this communication and create opportunities whenever possible. Employing effective two-way communication will make it difficult for anyone to marginalize the school library or place the school librarian on the sidelines.

Funding and Budgets

Of all the impediments to the development of the school library, the budget seems to be one of the greatest. School libraries either thrive or are noticeably in decline based on the soundness of, or lack of, a financial plan. Although it is easy to bemoan the fact that if only more money were allocated to the school library most problems would be resolved, the fact is that if you want someone to provide funding, you need to provide a detailed prospectus and evidence about why the school library is worth the investment. The school library brand can play a significant role in supporting your case for funding and establishing how far-reaching an investment in the library can be.

If a school librarian is lucky enough to be invited to submit a budget to administration, there is reason to hope it will be supported; however, more often than not, school administrators make assumptions about how much money to allocate, and it is necessary for school librarians to step up and be counted. That means making certain that your decision makers realize that a school library cannot exist as it should if it is reliant on grant-seeking, fund-raising, or bookfair profits to subsist. All those means can supplement the school library budget, but they do not replace it. Your understanding of the budget cycle in your district and your financial planning and preparation for this undertaking will speak volumes about your brand and the choice to invest in the school library, an essential part of the school with a comprehensive impact on the learning community.

In tight economic times, it is more critical than ever to align the school library and its brand with the instructional and organizational goals of the learning institution it serves. Demonstrate those connections through strong documentation and presentation of evidence that will assist decision makers in understanding the learning dividends that result in the school library from appropriate levels of funding.

In addition to collecting traditional data to gauge use and value of the school library and its programs, applying a collection-development plan framework can be powerful when aligned with the budget and development of an annual budget summary. This framework can also augment your selection policy, further establishing your school library brand.

Staffing

Appropriate levels of school library staffing are a hurdle for many school libraries. New school librarians and seasoned veterans alike are fortunate to land in a school with sufficient staffing, including eager, hardworking, and pleasant paraprofessionals or clerks. Many of us are working solo with no clerical help or are trying to cover multiple schools in a district while each individual school library is actually maintained by a paraprofessional.

This gap was underscored in a presentation by Deb Kachel of Project SLIDE when she stated that "in 2018–19, almost half (47%) of districts that had no librarians reported some level of library support staff, library aides working without the supervision or guidance of a school librarian" (Kachel and Kaaland 2021).

Staffing gaps like these can be both the cause and the result of a suffering school library brand.

> The success of a school library, no matter how well designed, ultimately depends on the quality and number of personnel responsible for managing the instructional program and the school library's physical and virtual resources. A full-time certified school librarian, supported by dedicated technical and clerical staff, is crucial to an effective school library for a school's learning environment. Every learner, classroom educator, and administrator in every school building at every grade level should have access to a fully staffed school library throughout the school day. (AASL 2019a)

Volunteers can be somewhat of an auxiliary school library staff but, though well intentioned, are sometimes unreliable or overstep their bounds. Overcoming the hurdle of insufficient staffing for an active, rich school library program requires more supervision than your available time and can result in a brand of mismanagement instead of effective, exciting, and engaging immersion in student learning.

Personality

We cannot leave out of a discussion on barriers to a strong school library brand the "elephant in the room." That particular pachyderm is personality. We have seen that if administrators encounter a cranky librarian while growing up, all librarians in their orbit are marginalized—and that perception is a barrier to a welcoming, collaborative school library brand. That bias continues and, though we are wincing when writing this, sometimes for a reason.

Administrators' Perceptions

In her doctoral dissertation work, Allison Kaplan (2006) interviewed doctoral candidates in education administration and found that future administrators responded positively about statements related to staffing, scheduling, and the roles of school librarians. However,

> when asked in a follow-up question to identify obstacles to the implementation of exemplary programs, the most serious concern focused not on any technical competence, but rather on the personality of the librarian. The same concern surfaced in a study conducted by Roys and Brown (2004) in which "ability to work with others" was the top rated "quality" used by the school administrators they surveyed in hiring a school librarian. (Shannon 2009, 2)

Whose Library Is It Anyway?

It's not about you. It's about the school library and its primary audience, the learners. It's easy to spot a territorial school librarian. "It's *my* library, *my* rules, *my* budget." Nope, nope, nope. It's about the learners and their learning, their growth. In a blog post titled "10 Traits of Successful School Librarians," Doug Johnson identified a key trait:

> They own the responsibility for the effectiveness of the library program, but not the library itself. The librarians I respect most understand that the whole school "owns" the library, not them. They are the custodians of this jointly owned resource. All advocacy efforts have at their core WIIFMS (What's In It For My Students/Staff). They will never refer to where they work as "my library." (Johnson 2018)

Dispositions

Picture in your mind a person who meets the school community every day at the door of the library. That person conveys the personality and dispositions of the image that should immediately come to mind when the term *school librarian* is mentioned. That image—those dispositions—is your brand.

"School librarians catalyze change that creates college-, career-, and life-ready learners as well as passionate, innovative, and engaged citizens" (AASL 2018b, 44). Yes, there are tough situations in school libraries that should not exist. Budget changes because of a shortfall in district funding can mean that the smoothly running, collaborative program you developed over a period of years is shattered by cuts to staff and budget. That happened to Sara, twice. Job changes forced on you suddenly can shake your confidence. It's difficult to step back and say, "I can give it my best try," rather than "I can't do this. It's not fair." Mourn, reassess what you can hold on to versus what you must let go—and check your attitude. A morose personality is a barrier. Likewise, make sure that you are not exhibiting diva-like behavior traits. Nobody likes a know-it-all. A bit of modesty never hurts your brand.

Image

Closely related to personality is image and the fact that many of our stakeholders have a preconceived notion of a school librarian and librarians in general. We are prone to being labeled as schoolmarmish, noise-hating, self-righteous prudes. Whether this characterization is deserved or not, it is up to each of us to not feed into the stereotypical image and to do so without being perceived as a whiner.

Problem Solving versus Complaining

Sara recollects hearing the phrase, "Don't bring me your problems, bring me your solutions." The comment stayed with her, and she focused on being solution-oriented when she encountered a thorny issue. There is some pushback in the business world regarding the solutions versus problems approach. Sabina Nawaz noted as much in a *Harvard Business Review* blog post:

> Even though advocates of this approach believe it reduces whining, increases empowerment, helps employees manage up, and boosts careers, it's fraught with challenges. Not every problem has an easy solution. Tackling the complexity of most significant business issues can take a pool of talented people with diverse points of view. . . . The "bring me a solution" approach can also cause employees to shut down in fear, breed a culture of intimidation, and prevent some problems from surfacing until they're full-blown crises. (2017)

Susan found this out firsthand. Read on!

Communicate Your Status

As a district director, Susan realized that sometimes building-level school librarians were complaining about an issue but, simultaneously, were afraid to let her know about a problem. The librarians seemed to think that they had to address any difficulty on their own, when in fact she might be able to help. Susan came up with a device she called the Monthly Memo (see figure 6.3 for an example of a monthly memo). At first the school librarians *hated* it! Nonetheless, she required that they submit a memo in advance of each monthly department meeting. Susan sifted through the memos and sorted them into two categories: issues that she would need to address individually, and issues that the entire team could help solve. After a while, the memos became a way of doing business, and problems got resolved before they turned into

MONTHLY MEMO

NAME: **DATE:**

What went right this month?

What went wrong?

What might help to fix what went wrong?

Instructional strategies/projects I am excited about:

Assistance/resources that would help:

FIGURE 6.3

The Monthly Memo

insurmountable difficulties or potential brand image problems. The approach also turned the volume way down on that major image-buster—whining!

Think about using a tool like the monthly memo to communicate what is happening and to let others know that, though you are working to resolve issues, you may need some assistance. It sure beats the alternative of being perceived as a grouch! If you don't have a district supervisor, ask your principal if you can share a monthly memo to advise them of developments and make sure they have the whole picture. Whether presenting problems or solutions, a proactive approach will enhance your image and your brand.

Inadequate Resources

If a brand is the expectations that others have about you and your product or services, then a school library's resources are the foundation for its brand. The materials in the school library must support the curriculum and reflect learners' personal growth and education. A well-balanced school library collection will communicate a brand for itself—learners will know that the school librarian selects high-quality materials at all reading levels just for them; classroom educators will know that their learners have easy access to materials that support their subject areas; administrators and school boards will know how important it is to support the school library's resources with adequate funds to make that all happen. Wait! Sadly, that last one does not happen for every school library. Many schools are underfunded, or the library collection has been neglected for years. Although we hope that the situation in your school library is not as dire, every school librarian needs to be proactive to ensure that their collection-development plan embodies the national standards, is data-driven and evidence-based, and reflects and empowers your learners. It's not fair, but a shabby collection is reflected in the perception of your brand.

Planning for Growth

The Domains of the *National School Library Standards* frameworks define what we want learners to be able to do—Think, Create, Share, and Grow—while demonstrating their Competencies in meeting the Shared Foundations of Inquire, Include, Collaborate, Curate, Explore, and Engage. Any school librarian needing to create a strong collection-development plan to improve the quality of a library's resources can create that plan's foundation with the AASL Standards as its cornerstone. In addition, school or district curriculum and the national standards that apply to subject areas and other educators in your school should be considered in your collection planning.

RESOURCES FOR MAPPING YOUR BRAND GROWTH

As you move along your journey of professional growth and brand development, using a personal growth plan to assess your strengths and identify areas for improvement is essential. These resources offer tools and structures as valuable guides.

"Measuring School Librarian Growth," chapter 13 in the *National School Library Standar ds for Learners, School Librarians, and School Libraries* (AASL 2018b)

This chapter will help you link your professional activities to the AASL Standards Frameworks and collect evidence through formative and summative evaluation. Once you have a library of evidence, consider ways to showcase selections from it for your learning community. Formal data, anecdotal reports, and material examples can give visibility and shape to strong messages for your school library brand.

School Library Professional Standards for Educational Leaders (SLPSELs; ALA 2022a)

A valuable resource for mapping your brand growth, these school librarian competencies, based on the PSELs originally developed by the National Policy Board for Educational Administration, provide additional direction for individual growth, offering rubrics, resources, and strategies related to advocacy, value, measurability, and more.

AASL offers a growing and evolving set of crosswalks between the *National School Library Standards* and other sets of national standards as a tool to assist with making these connections.

Also post your collection-development policy on your website to be more transparent and help the public better understand the significant, thoughtful process that goes into collection development. Using AASL Standards and content-area standards will help you become more articulate about your collection, exponentially strengthen your brand in the eyes of classroom educators and administrators, and solidify your image as a professional.

Weeding for Growth

As critical as it is to have a selection policy endorsed by your school board, you also need a policy that outlines the removal of materials when in poor condition, outdated, or unread, or when the information is not correct. School library collections need to accurately reflect our communities' experiences and history, embrace a wide variety of points of view, and include materials that help learners develop empathy for all people. A regularly weeded collection offers room for growth—for materials, for learners, for other educators, and for your school library brand.

Lack of (or Too Much) Professional Development or Continuing Education

If being a successful school librarian were as easy as completing a preparation program and finding a position, we'd all be considered top-notch! However, without ongoing professional development and continuing education, all the preparation in the world will not equip us to sustain the level of practice that is needed to be effective, have a positive impact in our communities, and grow the overall school library brand.

Standards as the Compass

Continuous improvement is the name of the game, and, in our quest to refine our brand, it is essential to annually take stock of strengths and weaknesses in the school library aligned with the needs of *our* community. Notice the emphasis on the word *our*. This is because it is too easy to get distracted by what someone else is doing for *their* school library and think that we must follow their lead, but does it actually work for *your* community or *your* brand? Of course, there are elements and aspects of school librarianship that we should all strive to focus on—and they are clearly delineated for us in the *National School Library Standards*. This is our foundational work developed for the profession, by the profession, and it makes use of deep thinking, research, and best practices to move us all forward.

Finding a Focus

It is clear that not engaging in continuing education is a barrier to your professional growth and the growth of your school library and its brand. However, overindulging in professional development can also interfere with your growth. It is important to spend time reflecting on your knowledge, skills, and dispositions, and on your community's needs, to narrow and prioritize your goals and to find the right balance to make effective use of your time and limited resources. Make it count and then make room to apply what you've learned.

In addition to face-to-face opportunities presented at state and national conferences, there are an endless number of webinars, Twitter chats, virtual meetups, and the like that could well demand too much of your time. Our advice is to first turn to state and national professional associations that are the most likely to have learning opportunities aligned with the standards and, thereafter, only those providers that you know are interested in advancing the profession. Think of the Latin phrase *Cui bono?* Who benefits from your participation in an event? Does the event involve peers or experts that you respect? Or is it market-driven and commercially motivated, anticipating your patronage for a product or service? There is a difference, so be a discerning consumer. Select opportunities that are designed to further school libraries and help you grow your brand, not theirs.

Questions for the Reflective Practitioner

1. How can you change your circulation and fine policies to be more supportive of student literacy?

2. Once unique barriers are identified, how do you market the need for change with the stakeholders identified in the AASL personas, and in your own personas, while promoting your brand?

3. In addition to observational notes, what data and evidence might you use to evaluate how users interface with the school library facility?

4. What forms of two-way communication would assist you to avoid marginalization and at the same time develop improved support for funding the staffing and resource needs of the school library?

5. What personality type do your students find when they open the door, virtually or physically? How can you give yourself an "attitude and image adjustment"?

6. Does your collection-development plan include improving the diversity and currency of your resources?

7. What are some ways in which you can establish priorities for professional development/ continuing education?

Extreme Makeover

If you have more than three priorities, you have none.
—Tony Wagner (addressing the Londonderry,
New Hampshire, School Board, 1997)

To develop a variety of strategies to overcome the many barriers to building a strong school library brand, it is important to consider experiences and perspectives beyond our own. Using the fictitious Gaver City School Library Department, let's explore some problems, situations, and solutions developed by the impacted school librarians and analyze their effectiveness. How do the AASL Standards integrate with the choices made based on the examples in the brand challenges? As we evaluate the mock school library department, its brand, and customer impressions, we emphasize the importance of being strategic and focusing on the *most immediate areas* for change.

The Facts

Gaver City is a midsized city in the Northeast and serves a diverse community of approximately 115,000 people and 12,500 students. Gaver City was once the site of the national headquarters of a well-known manufacturing company, and during that time the school system flourished. In fact, it was considered the "jewel in the crown" among all the school systems in the state, but that was then, and this is now. Like many other cities in the region, Gaver City experienced a significant loss of jobs when the manufacturing company, which was so central to the local economy, decided to move operations elsewhere. The population dwindled, and so did the resources available to support the schools. Recently there has been a glimmer of hope with a high-tech resurgence in the community and an increasing number of younger families;

an influx of immigrants has followed these emerging industries to Gaver City. These "newbies" are demanding more of the school system, and because of their support, the city was able to pass a bond initiative to refurbish aging schools and facilities as well as restore positions and programs that had been eliminated over the years. This revitalization includes the School Library Department.

Snapshot of the School Libraries

Once a vibrant and important part of the picture, with one or two exceptions, the school libraries in the Gaver City School District have been hanging on, but overall, the collections and facilities are dated. There has been no one at the district level to coordinate efforts, so policies and procedures are a bit of a hodgepodge, and because of site-based management, there is no consistency among the schools on budget and equity concerns. Additionally, though Gaver City was able to continue to provide the services of a certified school librarian at each of its schools, there are significant gaps in the level of support staff, with some schools in better shape than others. The librarians at the four high schools, three middle schools, and fourteen elementary schools must rely strictly on the goodwill of volunteers.

Such is the situation when Margot Markuson, the newly hired supervisor of the school libraries, arrives in Gaver City. She is not the only new face to the program. When it was announced that Margot would be heading up the program, a long-time high school librarian who had been one of the finalists for the position, and who was widely expected to get the job, resigned and left behind several colleagues who are none too happy about their new supervisor.

Identifying Brand Barriers and Making Assessments

Margot decided that the first thing she must do is mend fences with the staff and assure them that she is respectful of their work, as well as reliant on their institutional memory and experiences to find out what is needed in Gaver City. She recognized, and said so, that they had the knowledge base that was going to serve as the cornerstone of a new school library era in Gaver City. She scheduled time with each staff member for a one-on-one conversation before she brought them together as a group. During individual meetings she asked what their greatest concerns were and specifically asked them about issues related to the various brand barriers typically encountered.

Margot asked each of the school librarians to fill out the *National School Library Standards* School Library Evaluation Checklist (AASL 2018b, 174–180) before the upcoming meeting of district librarians. When the librarians gathered, they began to rank-order brand barriers that the group agreed should be addressed in the district overall.

However, realizing that their individual school communities should also have a say in what was to be a rebranding of their school libraries, the librarians collectively determined that a needs assessment at each school was necessary to move forward. The group expanded the School Library Evaluation Checklist to include additional items that they felt were important, such as the organization and discoverability of resources, communications and outreach, and instructional assessment. They developed a Likert scale (0 = *Nonexistent*, 1 = *Poor*, 2 = *Fair*, 3 = *Good*, 4 = *Excellent*). The librarians then asked their building administrators and key faculty to complete the expanded checklist (appendix B). In the interim, Margot asked all the school librarians to review AASL's National School Library of the Year award rubric and complete the sections for School Profile, Digital Profile, Staffing Profile, Expenditures Per Pupil, and Collection Report to reveal how each school library was performing (figure 7.1).

FIGURE 7.1

National School Library of the Year award rubric

School(s) Profile			Percent Enrollment by Special Groups			Percent Enrollment by Ethnicity				
School	Number of Pupils	Ratio of Students to Librarians	Economically Disadvantaged	English Learner	Special Education	White (Not Hispanic)	Black or African American (Not Hispanic)	Hispanic	Asian	Other

Digital Profile

School Website	
Library Website	
Social Media (ID Format)	
Social Media (ID Format)	
Social Media (ID Format)	
Social Media (ID Format)	

(continued)

FIGURE 7.1

National School Library of the Year award rubric *(continued)*

Staffing Profile

Grade Levels	Number of Schools in Local Educational Agency	Number of Pupils in Local Educational Agency	Certified School Librarians			Support Staff		
			Full Time	Half Time	Less than Half Time	Full Time	Half Time	Less than Half Time

Expenditures Per Pupil for Library Resources (Print and Digital Resources)

	Current Year (Insert Year)	Last Year (Insert Year)	Previous Year (Insert Year)
Local Funds	$	$	$
State Funds	$	$	$
Federal Funds	$	$	$
Endowments/Other	$	$	$
Total	$	$	$

Collection Report

Print Collection		Percent of Collection	Format Statistics				
Size	Avg. Age of 600s	Written in a Language Other Than English	Digital Subscription Resources	Audio Books	Electronic Books	Other Formats

Follow-up meetings between each school librarian and their building-level completers were scheduled. These meetings not only led to the identification of areas of mutual and immediate concern but also helped educate others, including administrators and school board members, about the school librarian's roles and responsibilities and the expectations that all schools should have for their school librarian. The entire school community was able to see the side-by-side comparisons among the schools related to demographics and the distribution of resources and staff. Priority areas were identified to start the renewal and rebranding of the School Library Department and each school library.

Brand Challenge 1:
Circulation Policy Review for Strengthening Literacy

In response to the School Library Evaluation Checklist, the new principal at E. Blanche Woolls Elementary School noted that test scores showed the need for students to strengthen their literacy skills. The school library's participation in that effort should include increased access to books. The long-time circulation policy needed to be examined. Currently, kindergarten learners can take out one book at a time—but it must remain in their classroom. First-graders can sign out one book and take it home. With each subsequent grade level, the total number of books increases—but a forgotten or lost book means that learners lose the possibility of signing out any books until it is returned or paid for.

Helen, an experienced school librarian in her second year at Woolls, is ready to tackle a policy revision but suspects that she will get pushback from her paraprofessional and some of the classroom educators. Helen sees the opportunity to elevate the school library's brand to one of strengthening literacy rather than being punitive toward student learners. She must make that case.

Helen researched fines, literacy, and school libraries and found a 2021 *School Library Journal* article reporting on a poll of librarians about fines and late fees (Cockcroft 2021). This article provided the support and data she needed to propose eliminating fines. Fines are a barrier, often for the student learners and their families who need access the most. Staff time for handling fines often took away time that could be used for other library tasks and provided less time for positive interactions with learners. That concept helped get the support of the paraprofessional in the school library.

Knowing that learners who read more achieve more, Helen turned to a U.S. Department of Education (n.d.) report, *Access to Reading Materials*, to document the need for children to have access to print reading materials for better academic outcomes. In this report, she found that 13 million children are enrolled in districts where materials circulation is less than ten books per learner, including 3.4 million students in poverty and 6.6 million students of color. Helen brought her research to the principal with a proposal to increase circulation:

- Allow more books per learner to be signed out by abolishing the book limit, which also gives Helen and the paraprofessional an opportunity to help learners case-by-case show respect for school library resources.
- Stop charging fines. Handling fines and late fees involves too much staff time for too little return. A notice and personal conversation often are much more effective.
- Develop a 3Rs policy—Return, Renew, or Replace. If a book is lost for more than ten weeks, learners may contribute the cost of replacement or donate books usable in the school library. A fourth R can be Refund if a book is eventually found. On occasions when learners cannot afford to pay for a missing book or donate a suitable book, the policy is to let it go. An automatic block on a learner's record in the circulation system can be removed by a keystroke and applied with equity and inclusion.

Helen presented her proposal at a general faculty meeting, answering questions from other educators with statistics from her research. The consensus was to try the proposed policy as outlined and evaluate the data at the end of the school year. Helen, her on-board principal, and the paraprofessional are sure that the new policies will make a difference, adding a focus on literacy to the school library's brand.

Brand Challenge 2: Preparing Advocates for Intellectual Freedom

Noah moved from an elementary school to the Lucille Cole Thomas Middle School and, two weeks into the school year, received a call from a sixth-grade parent objecting to a book. Additionally, a volunteer in the school library appeared to be censoring information resources related to controversial subjects. Prepared to address the issues, Noah also noted that two intellectual freedom concerns in such a short period of time may be a red flag for a brand barrier.

Noah had an "elevator speech" ready for the parent who called and for any parent who came to him with an informal challenge: "How wonderful that you know what your child is reading!" Noah was prepared with a gentle but firm follow-up statement if needed: "Every parent has the right to decide what is appropriate for their child to read but does not have the right to decide what other parents' children can read." Noah advised the parent who called him that the library circulation system can include notes from parents. He suggested that having a chat with their child about that feature could forestall a lot of problems. Noah shared details of the conversation with Margot, the district library supervisor, and his principal as a problem that seemed to be resolved.

The conversation also presented an opportunity for Noah to discuss the role of the school library with all his volunteer staff—a conversation he also shared with Margot. Noah emphasized to staff the need for the library to have well-curated information on *all* sides of a controversial issue and informed the volunteers that he expects their personal opinions will not be obvious to learners. He will, however, be quietly documenting any problems with this directive.

Although impressed with how Noah responded, Supervisor Margot also identified intellectual freedom as a potential brand weakness that may be affecting more school libraries in the district. She decided that it would be a good idea to review librarians' core value of intellectual freedom at the next department meeting, reminding school librarians and emphasizing that they report any conversation, civil or difficult, to her and their building principals. At the meeting, the librarians reviewed district policies and procedures as well as ALA and AASL materials supporting school libraries. Everyone bookmarked the ALA Office for Intellectual Freedom's (ALA/OIF) website and reviewed the procedures for reporting challenges to OIF. Margot reminded them that using ALA resources, including the Unite Against Book Bans (UABB) Toolkit, can often stabilize the situation when there is an informal or formal challenge. OIF can also provide help when needed, including legal assistance (ALA 2022b).

After reviewing the materials, the school librarians decided that the best way to develop the supporters and advocates each library needs for countering intellectual freedom challenges was to develop building-level library advisory committees to work on recommending policies, setting goals, and speaking up for the school library brand. The group discussed who should be represented on the advisory committees. Suggestions included administrators, board members, classroom educators, school staff, student learners, volunteers, community members, and other librarians from local academic and public libraries. Feeling prepared before a serious challenge means that each school librarian can break through the barrier of personal fears, develop the needed courage, and gain the trust of the learning community, ready to face intellectual freedom challenges with a team. The school library brand will be enhanced and sustained by their integrity and professionalism.

Brand Challenge 3:
Website Review for Visibility and Consistency

During the pandemic, the school library website was the virtual presence of the school librarian for learner access to resources like databases and e-books and to curbside pickup of print books. Postpandemic, school library websites continue to be portals for learners and classroom educators to connect with school librarians. However, district supervisor Margot realized that the Gaver City school library web access was not as visible as it should be. There is neither a link on the district main site to all libraries nor a link to the individual school library website when a particular school is selected. In addition, the appearance and organization of the school library websites are inconsistent depending on the web proficiency of each school librarian. Margot recognized that many brand barriers would remain without elevating and streamlining the online presence of school libraries in the district. But remodeling and aligning this variable brand experience with all school libraries online would require the support and participation of many individuals. Time for action!

Margot led the school librarian team as they conducted a study on good library websites and their characteristics. Team members developed a list of the features that should be present on each site, understanding the need for elementary, middle, and high school sites to look and work differently. During their research, the librarians greatly appreciated the resources and advice on the Librarians tab of the *SchoolLibraryNJ* LibGuide developed for Dr. Joyce Valenza's students at the Rutgers School of Communication and Information (Valenza 2022). They were especially inspired by Dr. Valenza's essay, "Your Library Website: It's a Destination, Not a Brochure!" (2022).

With the information gathered, the librarians came to consensus on the items each library would use as a guideline for its website's revisions, with customization for grade levels and specific needs for each school community:

- Very obvious link to their online public access catalogs (OPACs) and, vice versa, a link to the libraries' websites on their OPACs
- Links to public libraries
- Links to subscription databases (state- and district-purchased) with a login and federated search function
- Within the style parameters of the new department-developed website template, use of consistent colors and age-appropriate images (with alt text) to show that users are "in" the library
- Library calendar sign-up for educator collaboration
- Guides to new and carefully curated resources to build excitement for reading and learning
- Resource guides for collaborative projects
- Parent/community resources

- Links to resources for learner creation
- Space to highlight learner projects
- Hours (school day and 24/7!) and contact information for staff
- Policies and procedures for circulation and requests for materials reconsideration

Margot met with district administration to present the librarians' research and garner support for the project. She then met with the IT department to present the visibility and design priorities identified collectively by the group. School librarians met individually with IT staff to discuss customizations for specific school communities. After working through the process to redesign and relaunch the school library websites, the IT department provided in-service training for every school librarian on managing and updating website content. Now only *two* clicks from the school district's landing page, the school librarians were ready to open their virtual doors, presenting visitors a visible, dependable, professional perception of their brand.

Brand Challenge 4: Facility Audits for Brand Appearance

One of the first things Margot did after she was hired was to meet with each school librarian on their home turf, allowing her to connect in a more personal way as she introduced herself and found out about their concerns. Visiting the schools also allowed Margot to quickly eyeball the school library facilities and get an idea of the first impression each conveyed of the school library brand. In general, they presented a traditional look, with a worn-out, tired, and somewhat disorganized appearance. There was no consistency in signage, no real rhyme or reason for the placement of service areas, and she concluded that some of the veteran school librarians, as well as their respective school community members, may have just grown so accustomed to the environment that they had no idea how unattractive and uninviting the space had become.

A Picture Is Worth a Thousand Words

Because the school librarians were becoming used to Margot's "homework," as they called it, they were not surprised (although there was some grumbling about time constraints) when she asked them to take photos of various activities in and uses of their school library facilities. She gave the librarians particular assignments, such as taking a snapshot of a group of learners collaborating on a project or engaged in individual work or study, classroom educators instructing or interacting with their class in the library space, signs that offered directional assistance, displays that highlighted events or collection resources, and so on. "I also want you to maintain a journal and record what was happening when you took the photo," she directed, "so that you can help the team understand the context because we are all going to spend time analyzing the photos and what they might tell us." True to her word, the next department meeting was focused on looking at everyone's photos, first in small groups to sort similar situations and brand barriers. Each group then selected the most compelling photo to present to the entire team, sharing their analysis and possible solutions.

Improving Brand Appearance

Now that the school librarians realized there was work to do in terms of improving facility function and brand appearance, Margot introduced them to the concept of conducting a facility audit and provided them a simple tool to use to get an even better sense of what needed attention (figure 7.2).

FIGURE 7.2

Facility audit: Observation, data, and evidence

	Not evident		Could be improved		Represents the brand	
	✖	Notes	!	Notes	✔	Notes
Signage						
Clearly visible						
Attractive						
Easily understood						
Thoughtfully placed						
Uses empathetic messaging						
Uses symbols and nonverbal cues for English language learners						
Consistent in style						

	Not evident		Could be improved		Represents the brand	
	✖	Notes	!	Notes	✔	Notes
Layout						
Quiet zone						
Collaborative zone						
Flexible furnishings						
Seating options						
Production zone						
Workspace zone						
Space for collection						
Space for technology						
Instructional zone						
ADA compliant						
Intellectual Access						
Resources are organized for discoverability						
Resources are merchandized						
Standard nomenclature is in place						
Learner variabilities are addressed						
Use and Scheduling						
Accessible before and after school						
Use for nonlibrary purposes is minimal						
Schedule is responsive to the needs of learners						

As with the initial needs assessment using the School Library Evaluation Checklist, Margot directed the librarians to share the audit tool with their building administrators and to ask several classroom educators to participate. And because learner input was also vital, Margot developed criteria and a script for the librarians to use with a student focus group to gather learner impressions of how they interacted with the facility. Once the school librarians had analyzed all the elements and related input, it would be important for each of them to follow up with their audit participants, share the results, and let participants know what actions would be taken. Engaging stakeholders in the facility audit and following up to share results were just as important for improving school library brand perception as were the facility changes themselves.

Brand Challenge 5:
Changing Perceptions for Brand Rehabilitation

At Violet Harada High School, Inez has her work cut out for her! She is the replacement for Shamdie, who resigned after not getting the position of supervisor. Regrettably, Shamdie sowed the seeds of discontent not only among some of the other school librarians but also among some support staff and faculty at Harada. Inez decided, with Margot's support, to "ease into the position" and try not to make too many assumptions. It was important to get the lay of the land and understand the backstory before making changes or upsetting the status quo.

However, despite the cold shoulder from some faculty, and an initial bit of attitude from the library paraprofessional, it did not take long before other faculty and even administrators shared that they were not sorry to see her predecessor go! By mid-year Inez had learned that Shamdie had a very possessive attitude about the school library—or "my library" as she referred to it—and enforced some rather onerous "policies" with gusto, such as allowing only four learners at a table, admonishing (embarrassing) learners if they had forgotten a pen or pencil or had an overdue item, requiring that all books and other materials be returned before any vacation or holiday recess, and not allowing use of the school library for the first and last two weeks of the school year. Shamdie was also what one assistant principal called a "time bandit" who liked to wax on about copyright laws, delinquent borrowers, and unruly, ungrateful learners whenever he poked his head in the school library—which is why he had taken to avoiding the place. One department head confessed that though she knew she should involve the school librarian from the get-go as they revised curriculum, Shamdie was too much of a drag in department meetings. She always made the content-area educators feel that her skills were superior to theirs. They just didn't like her telling them how special she was.

Inez had previously known about her predecessor only through professional circles, where Shamdie was held in high regard. Harada High School was the one school in the system that had made progress over the years—with a fairly up-to-date facility and resources—while the others were stuck in a time warp. Shamdie was widely known as an "award-winning super star." She had been very active in several library associations, published in various journals, and had a very robust social media presence. However, it seems in her own backyard, she was viewed not as a team player but as a self-promoting glory hog. The assistant principal noted that "Shamdie was pretty high maintenance. The signature block of her e-mail included every award received and position held, and I just didn't get why she had to be constantly reminding us of her bona fides." Inez realized that though there were many positive legacy elements that she could attribute to Shamdie, including a significant impact on the profession at large, maintaining a positive image of the school library brand at home was not one of them.

Inez knew she had to rehabilitate the school library brand, which was clearly linked to the perception of Shamdie among many of the learners, faculty, and administrators. Because Margot had instituted the use of a monthly memo to help all the school librarians reflect on what was foremost on their minds related to their practice, Inez decided to use it to collect her thoughts and consider some strategies to move forward (figure 7.3 on the following page).

Brand Challenge 6:
Data Mapping for Vibrant Collections

Last year, Helen, a seasoned school librarian, was asked to step into the position of school librarian at Woolls Elementary School to cover a lengthy leave of absence. When she first arrived, she walked into the school library and immediately noticed that the books on the shelves were old and falling apart. A few classroom educators stopped by to welcome her and said, "Good luck with this place." Running an audit of the library management system to get to the bottom of the problem, she discovered that the average copyright date in the collection was 1987 and that there was a high percentage of lost and unreturned books. Helen also discovered that the previous principal had zeroed the school library budget as one of his site-based management decisions. Helen was at a loss, literally and figuratively, but she hung in and did her best with what little she had—which many school librarians do.

Fast-forward to this year and Woolls's new principal, Leon, who wants improved literacy and is ready to increase Helen's budget but wants the budget increase supported by data through a budget evaluation and summary so that he can justify an

MONTHLY MEMO

NAME: Inez Gordon   **DATE:** January Dept. Meeting

What went right this month?

The assistant principal (AP) and the Humanities Department head (DH) let me know that they were pleased to see that the school library seems more welcoming and kid-friendly.

What went wrong?

I indicated that we were hoping for better utilization but struggled with getting classroom educators to work with me on collaborative projects, etc. The AP and DH noted some lingering reticence due to negative experiences in the past and shared some personal encounters with me.

What might help to fix what went wrong?

I reconnected with the AP and DH and asked them to review proposed changes related to circulation, an issue in the past.

I need to strategize about the best ways to communicate to everyone that the school library is *their* resource, not mine. A survey to solicit input?

Instructional strategies/projects I am excited about:

Not instructional, but the AP was enthusiastic about the proposed changes and invited me to share with the Admin Team at their meeting. He said "This is really a step in the right direction—especially not requiring books to be returned before vacations!" I emphasized that I would need to make sure that any changes pass muster with the School Library Department before we take that step, and he was fine with waiting.

Assistance/resources that would help:

I think we need consistent circulation guidelines in the district to provide maximum access to school library materials. I would appreciate your support of a district-wide review of what is happening and the creation of a department subcommittee to make recommendations.

I would also like to meet and work with you to develop a survey for learners and educators to find out what they need, want, and expect from the school library.

FIGURE 7.3

Monthly Memo: Inez Gordon

increase to the superintendent and school board during this current school year. Change needs to happen right away, not next year. Helen is ready to tackle the work—data mapping and budgeting for a school library brand revival through a vibrant collection—and is thrilled to be working with a principal who is ready to advocate for the school library brand at the district level.

Helen decided that she will talk to her colleague Noah, who recently moved from an elementary school library with a good budget to a middle school library, and then visit other district schools that Noah recommends as having vibrant collections. Noah suggests an October 18, 2022, *Knowledge Quest* blog post by Leanne Ellis that inspired him. Its message resonated with both Noah and Helen—too often the books in a library seem to be the books that learners are *supposed* to read (subject-specific nonfiction, classics, award winners, and biographies) but not what they *want* to read. Noah suggested that Helen consider surveying learners about their reading interests, genrefying the library, and merchandising books as she develops an updated collection. Inspired, Helen starts her work to give Leon the data he needs to restore her budget this year.

Curriculum Map

To update the curriculum mapping the district did a few years ago and make it library focused, Helen developed a short online survey for faculty, explaining that she was working to update the school library's collection. The survey asked educators about their existing projects and about the types of books and online subscription databases they suggest for learner access through the school library.

Collection Map

Using the Curriculum Map Evaluation Worksheet (figure 7.4 on the following page) from Mona Kerby's *An Introduction to Collection Development for School Librarians* (2019), Helen mapped the current collection. With information from her curriculum survey and her circulation system's report, Helen identified the gaps and copyright dates for fiction, nonfiction, graphic novels, and alternate formats. Helen also recorded an evaluation for each faculty-identified topic. She knew that she would add more to the "Number of Items to Weed" column when she did physical weeding, finding books that were shabby or had out-of-date information.

Weeding/Deselection Policy

Despite not knowing whether the emergency budget request would be approved, Helen consulted the library department's weeding/deselection policy to remove the outdated and shabby books that she knew were just taking up space on the overcrowded bookshelves. As each book was deleted from the online catalog, Helen noted the reason for removal, producing a final report that documented her work. After three months of work, Helen ran a collection audit and was quite gratified to see the collection's average date at 2002, already in the current century! With the extra shelf space, Helen was ready to begin genrefying the collection.

Curriculum Map Evaluation Worksheet

Use this evaluation worksheet to map and analyze your collection against the different topics present in your school or district curriculum.

  A Column—Select a section to evaluate, not the entire collection. You might choose Fiction, 500s–600s, or 900s. You could be more specific and choose 599 Animals or 917 Geography, or you could select topics from the curriculum chart you created.

  B Column—Identify the grade level needed for the topic.

  C Column—Decide the level of support needed—minimal, basic, or extensive.

  D Column—Insert the number of items in the section.

  E Column—Insert the average copyright year for the items in the section.

  F Column—Determine the percentage of titles recommended by either H. W. Wilson or *Booklist* by taking a random sample and then looking up the reviews.

  G Column—Determine how many items to weed.

  H Column—Determine how many items to purchase, depending on available quality or new titles.

A	B	C	D	E	F	G	H
Dewey Number or Curriculum Subject	Grade Level	Level of Support	Number of Items	Average Copyright Year	Percentage of Positively Reviewed Titles	Number of Items to Weed	Number of Titles Recommended for Purchase

FIGURE 7.4

Curriculum Map Evaluation Worksheet

Source: Kerby 2019.

Diversity Audit

Helen knew the documentation from a diversity audit would be important for making her case to update materials. She studied the demographics of the school, important given increased immigration in the past ten years. She needed to represent these populations, including materials in their native languages. Helen also knew the importance of representing cultures not in the school to help learners increase their global awareness and empathy.

Collection-Development Plan

Helen used another template from Kerby (2019) to help document collection gaps and then determined the funding needed over three years to fill those gaps, as well as the ongoing funding needed to continue developing a print-rich collection (including e-books and other formats). As promised, she prioritized areas noted by the other educators who returned her curriculum map survey, as well as carefully curated materials to increase diversity, equity, and inclusion areas noted in the diversity audit. Helen then sent the budget request to supervisor Margot and principal Leon, asking for emergency funds to begin to update the collection this year. Margot and Leon then submitted the request to the superintendent and the school board.

Next, Helen outlined targeted purchases for the following two years of her three-year plan. Although she still sought supplemental grants and pursued fund-raising opportunities, Helen crafted a detailed, practical plan for a solid, deep collection with reasonable district budget expectations. As school library use, circulation, and literacy slowly began to rise with the refreshed collection, so did perceptions of the school library brand among administration, other educators, and learners.

Brand Challenge 7:
Big-Picture Planning for Resource Equity

At the top of Margot's to-do list after coming on board was the immediate need to develop and present a financial plan for the School Library Department for the following school year. Presenting a district-wide plan rather than individual library plans would help document the current inequitable distribution of resources (including personnel). It would also establish the importance of developing a forward-thinking blueprint addressing the imbalance as it impacts the brand perception of school libraries. Helen's recent data-backed budget win would be a fitting prelude to the big-picture conversation Margot would have with the school board.

Assembling a district-wide financial plan was a heavy lift because of Margot's limited background knowledge about what was already in place. However, using the data that the school librarians provided through the completion of AASL's School Library Evaluation Checklist (AASL 2018b, 174–180) and the National School Library of the Year Award Rubric (AASL 2021), Margot was able to get an overall feel for existing budgets and funding needs at individual school libraries and move forward. She also asked each school librarian to submit a needs-based budget using the categories in a provided budget request form (figure 7.5).

After meeting with each school librarian and their respective principal to review the requests, adjustments were made, and a final proposal was prepared. Margot enlisted Helen, as a seasoned and respected member of the department, to help her populate a narrative Budget Summary Framework (appendix C). This framework was designed to provide an overview of the importance of the school library brand in the big picture by aligning the vision, mission, and goals of the program with those of the schools and district. It also defined roles and responsibilities, highlighted challenges facing the brand, and prioritized strategies to address those challenges, including expected outcomes and performance indicators/deliverables. Margot and Helen then shared the interim framework with the other librarians in the district, giving them an opportunity to make suggestions and modifications before the document was finalized for the superintendent's review.

Brand Challenge 8: Staffing Comparisons for Equitable Service

On paper, Noah has a full-time paraprofessional to assist him. However, it doesn't feel that way to Noah. When he requested a transfer from an elementary school library position to the Lucille Cole Thomas Middle School, he expected that a well-regarded, experienced paraprofessional would be there to welcome him. However, because of a family situation, that paraprofessional resigned. Now, without any input, Noah is expected to train a new person hired by the principal (before Margot arrived). On top of that, tomorrow the first class of sixth graders is scheduled to be dropped off for library orientation. The art educator has e-mailed him about planning a collaborative project for her learners next week, which could be the beginning of collaboration, but he is also expected to make the school library available for seventh and eighth graders to sign out books.

To further complicate the situation, Noah learns from other educators that the principal frequently pulls the paraprofessional assigned to the school library for cafeteria coverage, special education aide, extra bus duty, and the like. Noah is beside himself. He shares his frustration with Margot, who responds, "I know you are overwhelmed, but we need to build a case and that means you are going to have to do some work—but the time and energy should yield results. Are you up for it? It seems

BUDGET REQUEST

School:	Date:	
	Request	**Current Allocation**
RESOURCES		
Print books—replacement and collection development		
E-books, audiobooks, and related services		
Periodicals—print and digital subscriptions		
Online databases and subscriptions		
Streaming media services		
Research management tools		
Online productivity tools		
Library Management System		
SUPPLIES		
Library		
Office		
Production—staff and student projects		
EQUIPMENT		
New		
Replacement		
FURNITURE		
New		
Replacement		
PROGRAMMING		
Displays		
Incentives		
Speakers		
PROFESSIONAL DEVELOPMENT		
Professional dues		
Conferences, webinars, etc.		

FIGURE 7.5

Budget request form

to me that your principal has a perception problem that is a barrier to your school library brand. He doesn't realize that when he pulls your paraprofessional, he is negatively impacting critical service to learners and classroom educators." Despite being frazzled, Noah agrees, and he and Margot enlist the two other middle school librarians to assist in the effort.

The three librarians begin to document how many hours a week their paraprofessionals actually work in the school library. After a month of data collection by the school librarians, Margot has enough to do a side-by-side comparison, and the results are startling! Margot pays a visit to the principal in question, noting that her monthly progress report to the superintendent is due and that before she finalizes it, she wants the principal to be aware that there is a significant gap in direct service to learners and educators at his school compared with the other middle schools. She tells him that she is worried that the superintendent may be upset given the district's equity agenda and that she feels that she should give the principal a heads-up. After looking at Margot's comparison, the very contrite principal asks her to "hold off" on including those data while he considers other means of coverage. "I admit, it has become a habit to just grab the library paraprofessional, mainly because it is convenient for me. I had not considered the impact on the learners and educators." Margot was happy to let the principal look for other options, while at the same time assuring him that when he was in a real coverage bind, of course school library personnel were there to help.

Brand Challenge 9: Professional Development and Continuing Education for Brand Growth

Whereas some of the school librarians have been supported in their participation in professional development activities outside the district, others have been unable to participate because of building schedules. Additionally, professional development (PD) and continuing education (CE) have not always been aligned with the strategic needs of the department, individual schools, or the district in general. By aligning PD/CE with strategic needs in the school and district, the school library brand is amplified. Because Margot is now the chief evaluator of the school librarians (in collaboration with their school principals), she checks in with other administrators to see whether the Gaver City Schools use an evaluation framework or instrument. She discovers not only that the district uses an evaluation framework that she is familiar with but also that the framework is highlighted in the *National School Library Standards*. This is good news! However, most of the principals had not used the instrument in school librarian evaluations because it was not adapted to the librarians' unique roles and responsibilities. Margot got busy creating a crosswalk using examples provided in the *National School Library Standards* (AASL 2018b, 155–163).

When the crosswalk was ready, Margot asked each school librarian to review it and develop a PD/CE plan based on self-assessment. It was important for Margot to get a snapshot of each school librarian's knowledge, skills, and dispositions related to the AASL Standards, as well as their progress connecting to building and district goals and objectives. She encouraged the school librarians to identify PD/CE opportunities that would support growth in targeted areas. As another means of appraising their own level of proficiency, Margot referred the librarians to *The Expert in the School Library: School Librarian–PSEL Competencies* (ALA 2022a), a self-assessment tool from ALA's Libraries Transform campaign. The school librarians were also asked to read appendix H, "Evidence of Accomplishment," in the *National School Library Standards* (AASL 2018b, 262) and checkmark items on the list that they could use to substantiate growth. Later, at a department meeting, the entire team considered whether there were still other "evidences" that could be added to the list. Margot then met with each school librarian, and they "negotiated" which PD/CE activities were most connected to their professional growth and to the needs of their learning communities as well as what evidence would best document the improvement.

Finally, Margot created a department PD/CE plan and calendar to share with the principals. The calendar indicated dates, places, and the time commitment required for school librarian participation in various conferences, workshops, webinars, and professional learning communities. It also noted whether the activity occurred during or after the school day and whether a cost was involved. She specified what benefits and improvements were expected because of participation, and how the school librarians could use their newfound proficiency to deliver in-house PD/CE for other educators. She also specified what evidence would be presented and analyzed to substantiate the investment in school librarian PD/CE and the school library brand. Providing this calendar to principals would reinforce the school librarian as an educator and position the school librarian brand as a resource for growing other educators.

Brand Challenges Summary

The Gaver City School Library Department faced a number of interesting and compelling brand challenges. However, by using the guidance and tools provided by the *National School Library Standards* in combination with other useful resources discovered through research and collaboration with one another, the school librarians were able to begin to develop solutions to address each challenge. The school library brand across the district and within each school is becoming stronger, more respected, and indicative of brand behavior that is centered on the district's learning communities and is memorable for positive engagement and experiences.

Questions for the Reflective Practitioner

1. If you do not have a library supervisor like Margot, you may need to develop an alliance with whomever your direct supervisor is. How would you approach that person for assistance?

2. How might you adapt the AASL Standards' School Library Evaluation Checklist for your own purposes?

3. How can you maximize working with other school librarians in your district to tackle brand barriers?

4. Was Margot's subterfuge fair in semi-outing the principal about his use of the library para-professional? What would you do in a similar situation?

5. How might you leverage your PD/CE to ensure maximum impact for your learning community?

Communications Plan

Every act of communication is a miracle of translation.

—Ken Liu (2016)

Throughout this book we have emphasized the importance of communication—two-way communication, that is! So why is it that so few school librarians take the time to develop an intentional plan to ensure that their communications are strategic and targeted to the right audiences? And on the flip side, why don't we provide a means for our audiences to likewise engage with and respond to our messaging with comments and input that will help strengthen the school library brand? Such was the conundrum facing the Gaver City School Library Department. As they coalesced as a team, the school librarians began to realize how much more effective they were together than when they tried to "go it alone." Small but impactful successes with budgets, policies, and staffing had made them identify more with one another and with their emerging brand. The librarians were proud to be members of a more unified team, which grew their desire to unify their brand. They wanted to ensure that they were delivering a similar message about the value of the school library as well as projecting a distinctive brand image that engendered respect. They realized that they needed to create a strategic communications plan.

We all must endeavor to do the same. The time and effort we put into providing exemplary services is crucial to learner achievement and success; the school library brand needs to be recognized for delivering consistent quality and excellence in that endeavor. A communications plan helps ensure that the good news about the school library is widespread, reaches the audiences you need it to, and is valued by those it serves.

School Library Communications Plan

A communications plan is designed to position your school library to be accountable to your learning communities and responsive to addressing their needs in the delivery of instruction and services. Initially, the plan should focus on increasing awareness of the value of the school library for various target audiences. Further, the plan must aim to develop an understanding of and commitment to the brand's value proposition with these audiences. Ultimately, the goal is to create a shared vision over time with stakeholders and constituents that will sustain the school library brand.

Establishing Your Brand with Target Audiences

Think about the personas we asked you to develop in chapter 2 and consider the needs of your particular stakeholders. We suspect that they are representative of the general audiences that school libraries serve and include parents, learners, other educators, principals and other administrators, school board members, legislators, other policymakers, and the broader community. Looking at the prime areas of interest for each target audience also provides focus when developing appropriate messaging. At the same time, it is important to recognize that the fine details for any school library or target audience may change over time, sometimes from message to message, and depending on the initiative or goal of the message. Periodically evaluating your audiences as well as your messaging goals is important for ensuring that your communications plan is effective.

- *Parents* need to know that their children are gaining improved literacy skills, are learning to love reading and learning, and are discovering the importance of critical thinking.
- *Learners* need to know that the school librarian will help them find what they need, whether it is pleasure reading or academic content—or even just information about which they are curious.
- *Other educators* are interested in how school library services benefit classroom curricula and help them improve their practice.
- *Principals and other administrators* need data and research that explain how school libraries and school librarians impact student achievement in positive ways.
- *School board members, legislators, other policymakers, and the broader community* also need data and research but may additionally need to better understand the role of the school library and what school librarians actually do (ALA 2022c).

Consider what your general target audiences *need to know* and the specific characteristics of the persona stakeholders in your learning community as you build your communications plan. With this lens, apply a three-pronged approach for establishing your school library brand:

1. Image building
2. Promotion and outreach via traditional means and planning for social media engagement
3. Strategies for continuous feedback, evaluation, and sustainability

Image Building

Image building requires time. It is a conscious effort to build and maintain a positive impression and recognition of the unique aspects of your particular product. In the instance of school libraries, our product is ensuring the ability of learners to successfully engage and interact with ideas and information. Brand look, taglines, messaging, and testimonials are all elements of image building.

Brand Look

In their book *Bite-Sized Marketing*, authors Nancy Dowd, Mary Evangeliste, and Jonathan Silberman (2010, pp. 122–123) note that the elements of a brand image are

- a logo,
- the use of no more than two fonts (one serif and one sans-serif),
- a color palette of three colors, and
- a style guide with specific requirements and options for all publications and communications.

The purpose of a style guide is to ensure consistency across brand messaging, materials, and content—also known as **brand collateral**. Developing the style guidelines should be a collaborative and consensual process. It should benefit both you as the content creator of school library messaging and your school or district as the umbrella organization. A school library brand style guide should include these elements:

- An editorial process—to ensure that content is checked for spelling, grammar, veracity, consistency, and compliance with school board policy before publication in any official communications channel.
- Specifications and visual examples for each element in the brand look—logo orientations and variations, fonts, color palettes, and the like.

- Preferred spellings and use of terms—for example, the AASL style guide indicates a preference for the use of the term *learner* versus *student* and *educator* versus *teacher*.
- Templates created for all publications used by school librarians—having a standard format for such items as press releases and website home pages helps to consistently convey and connect the brand look.

Tagline

Research tells us that school libraries are quality indicators of educator excellence and learner achievement in a school or district. This role is what we want school libraries to be known for and what makes us unique and distinctive. This focus should be represented in a tagline that addresses how we intend to deliver on the promise of the brand. A tagline, formerly referred to as a slogan or motto, reflects your brand and the association you want people to have when they hear or read it. A tagline needs to be succinct—a pithy soundbite that epitomizes your brand. Use it everywhere in your communications, but revisit and rethink it periodically to make sure it still reflects your evolving school library brand.

Sample school library tagline: "Ideas, information, and technology to lift learning to new heights."

Messaging

Brand messaging involves the expression of key strengths that speak to the school library brand and includes targeted messages for selected audiences. Messaging will help translate why our brand has value for each audience. In revisiting Jim Collins's *Good to Great and the Social Sectors*, we were reminded of the "hedgehog concept." This is the convergence of (a) what an organization is deeply passionate about, (b) what you can be the best in the world at, and (c) what drives your resource engine. Its essence is to gain "piercing clarity about how to produce the best long-term results, and then exercising the relentless discipline to say 'No thank you' to opportunities that fail the hedgehog test" (Collins 2005, 17).

For school libraries, brand messaging should focus on learner experiences and related outcomes. Review the key messages listed in the *School Libraries Transform Learning Message Box* (AASL 2022) found on the AASL Standards portal (standards .aasl.org) and identify those that would resonate most with your school library target audiences. For example, the following are those we felt were most connected to learner experiences:

- The school library is a unique and essential part of the learning community.
- School librarians are instructional leaders who provide a wide-angle lens on learning across all disciplines, grades, and abilities in the school community.
- The school library is the great equalizer for all learners.
- Every learner has the right to choose what they will read, view, or hear.
- An effective school library plays a crucial role in bridging digital and socio-economic divides.
- School libraries provide equitable 24/7 open access to resources and technological learning tools.
- School libraries create inclusive environments where all learners feel safe to create knowledge and share their perspectives.
- School libraries prepare all learners for college, career, and life.
- School libraries are learner-centered environments that foster inquiry and critical thinking.
- Reading is the core of personal and academic success.
- School library experiences prepare students to think, create, share, and grow as effective users and creators of ideas and information.

Although the remaining messages in the message box document are also important, focus at least initially on the school library and learners, reassessing messages annually.

Testimonials

Testimonials validate brand behavior. People appreciate recommendations and look for "likes." We have all checked out product reviews and ratings or added our thumbs up or thumbs down to indicate our impression of a brand. Testimonials from our satisfied customers serve the same purpose and can help influence others to appreciate the school library brand. These are the best proof that we have people of influence and substance who have witnessed and now believe in the transformational promise of school libraries.

How do you successfully solicit testimonials? Michael Zipursky (n.d.) of Consulting Success contends that the best way to get testimonials is to do these three things:

1. Do great work.
2. Ask.
3. Make it easy.

The first step is a given—we expect that school librarians do great work! However, it's only great work if people know about it, so you must take the second step and ask those target audiences for whom you have done that work to help you spread the word. Some of those audiences may respond well to an e-mail request with a survey or submission link. Others may need a face-to-face personal invitation from you to provide a testimonial. For instance, you can ask parents during open house nights or parent conferences. Or, when you successfully collaborate with a fellow educator, ask them to fill out a collaboration "exit ticket" testimonial. This statement not only documents the collaboration but also provides copy for a newsletter item. With any of your target audiences, suggest that their experience would be a good candidate for your predesigned plug-and-play video script.

All your audiences will be more inclined to participate if you provide prompts and cues that will help them frame their response. Although you will want to develop your own prompts related to your situation, questions such as "How has your learner benefited from the school library?" for parents or "What learner improvement did you observe as a result of collaboration with the school librarian?" for educators should assist them in sharing their positive perceptions of the school library brand. Or for fun, ask Pre-K–12 learners to contribute to a list of the Top Ten Reasons to Love Your School Library.

Not only should testimonials highlight the positive brand experiences of each type of school library target audience, but you must also think about the best way to deliver them—print, video, audio, online, and so on. Know your demographics. Here are some ideas:

- *Learners:* Provide opportunities for learners who have benefited from the school library to create video testimonials for their peers, delivered via social media platforms and the school library website.
- *Educator partners:* Consider a regular newsletter or web feature spotlighting those who have collaborated with the school librarian and can speak to learner impact.
- *Administrators:* Provide principals and other administrators with information about the positive contributions of the school library or librarian via monthly reports and invitations to participate in or observe school library happenings. Encourage them to use their newsletters, social media accounts, and web pages to distribute their insights about the same.
- *Parents and community members:* Connect with a parent, community member, or local business leader who collaborated with the school library and ask them to share their story. Distribute opt-in e-mailed or snail-mailed newsletters and include information on how to follow school library social media. A parent area on your school library website can also deliver testimonials and messages when parents go there to help their learners.

Promotion and Outreach

Promotion includes all public relations and media relations activities. The accomplishments of learners and educators need to be highlighted in relation to our school libraries, using vehicles and channels preferred by the audiences we are trying to reach. Media organizations, traditional communication vehicles, new media tools, and community outreach all offer opportunities to introduce and fortify your school library brand. Choices will depend on content, brand messaging, and targeted audience.

Media Relations

Mounting a media strategy campaign can also help position the school library brand. Through strategic use of the media, you can promote positive events and accomplishments related to the school library. Take advantage of local media attention—they love stories that feature local youth—and consider the following tactics when building your media strategy:

- Identify events and information that are appropriate for press releases.
- Create a press release template that includes your contact information. You may also need to include contact information for someone in the district media relations department, so be sure to check with them as well.
- Create and maintain an updated list of all local media contacts.
- Work with local media to create public service announcements (PSAs) that promote school library events and accomplishments.
- Meet with the community relations leaders of media outlets to form partnerships that can promote events.
- Develop and maintain an up-to-date resource guide for directing media outlets and inquiries to various district experts.
- Create and regularly update a yearly calendar of events to share with media contacts (include events such as Banned Books Week, Children's Book Week, School Library Month, etc.).

Community Outreach and Partnerships

Leverage local partnerships and strengthen ties to your local public library, any community colleges or universities, and community service and social organizations for their assistance in helping to push out messages and information about events—and reciprocate by highlighting theirs. Hosting community events in person and virtually, such as an open house for parents, helps position your brand as accommodating and welcoming. Likewise, invite your community partners to participate in an activity such as a Children's Book Week observance during which community members are invited to read to learners, or a college, trade, or career day that highlights and celebrates the expertise and experience of community members and organizations. Another way to connect within the greater community is to have a presence at community events, using display tables/stands, banners, and looping video presentations about school libraries, including testimonials!

Identify a contact person for each entity to include in press releases and the like. This person should also be your go-to for input and feedback regarding your efforts.

Traditional Communication Vehicles

All current materials should be reviewed for alignment with your style guide. If creating unique informational material feels overwhelming to you, then do not reinvent the wheel. AASL provides a variety of materials for distribution at the AASL Standards portal (standards.aasl.org), including one-pagers, infographics, and more targeted to a variety of audiences. Print them, link to them, or use them as inspiration to create custom materials for your community.

When it comes to deciding which vehicle to use for a particular target audience, it really depends on the message being conveyed—or as notably observed by Marshall McLuhan (1964), "the medium is the message." Each of the following communication vehicles has an advantage when it comes to determining what brand content might be shared through them, and certain target audiences may respond better to one vehicle or another.

- *Newsletters:* These are a reliable means of sharing information and featuring news about the school library brand. They can be distributed in print or digital form and work well for both internal and external audiences. A publication schedule can be established (weekly, monthly, quarterly) to ensure a regular, reliable stream of communication.
- *One-pagers:* These materials are helpful for emphasizing key messages for different audiences. For example, if learners have been struggling with citations, you might prepare a one-pager that you make available at the circulation desk, and another one-pager directed to parents to help their learner at home and that you distribute at an open house.
- *Program leaflets and brochures:* These publications are used to provide more detail about and promote a service or to answer specific questions regarding a variety of issues, such as the dos and don'ts of copyright or FAQs related to the school library and its resources or a detailed list of available online databases and tips on how to use them.
- *Posters and infographics:* These products help convey areas of focus visually and are appealing to visual learners and busy people. For instance, your monthly

or annual report to administrators is often more impactful as an infographic. Also you can convey the essence of what school libraries are about using this channel. To save time, consider using online creation tools like Canva, or search for ready-made school library infographics online. Of course, using data from your own learning community may be more powerful with your stakeholders, but AASL and other organizations and individuals have shared compelling infographics on school library and educational topics.

- *E-mail:* This is a great means of delivering targeted messages. E-mail blasts make it easy to connect with everyone on a particular distribution list (and you may have separate lists for each audience). Invites to an upcoming school library event, digital newsletters, or news about an award or recognition can easily be shared with your stakeholders via e-mail.
- *Website:* Not only does the school library website offer the first impression and first point of contact for many of your visitors, but in the long run, a strong website can deliver substantial cost savings by reducing or eliminating the distribution costs, like printing and postage, for other traditional communication vehicles.

Social Media Planning

School libraries should be promoting their brand on social media platforms, but it is important that school librarians first take the time to develop a social media plan that considers district social media requirements. Take the time to get the plan approved by administration before the first posts. School library social media should never reflect personal opinion, nor suggest political action, or cross over into individual social media accounts held outside school.

While crafting your social media plan, you will want to consider several questions. There are no right or wrong answers to these questions. Each school librarian or district library department will need to answer these questions for themselves based on their learning community and their district guidelines.

- What types of content best represent and build your school library brand?
- What social media platforms are most used by your audiences?
- Which types of messages are best distributed using those platforms?
- What platforms are you already comfortable using?
- Who will be in charge of posting?
- What will be the timing of the posts? Episodic or scheduled? Both?

You may also wish to spend some time considering how you will respond to common questions you may receive from administration when seeking approval of your social media plan.

- *Why do school libraries need to be on social media?* Social media offer a brand-building opportunity for school libraries to, among other things, market the resources available for learners, especially books in all formats. School librarians can also document events, such as school spirit day or school-wide food drives, and publicize learner inquiry projects by posting photos and videos. School library events like School Library Month and Children's Book Week can be advertised to build support, and the learning and the fun can be shared—of course, following district guidelines for using images of learners online. A school library YouTube account can provide the medium for tutorials on using resources, such as how to download e-books, as well as for testimonials from learners, educators, and parents. The school library's YouTube channel could also be used to provide professional development for other educators, thereby promoting the school library brand as a professional development resource. Consider issuing web badges and micro-certificates that would offer educators and learners the opportunity to digitally showcase their learning to their professional and social contacts and communities, further spreading awareness of the school library brand.

- *What are the ages of our potential followers? What platforms do they use?* For many social media platforms, usage statistics are available that can verify who is viewing posts, in addition to tracking "likes" and comments. All the audiences identified earlier are likely to be using social media and are possible followers, but the annually updated Pew Research Center social media fact sheet helps to better define usage. For instance, the 2021 Pew *Social Media Fact Sheet* shows that more than 80 percent of people between the ages of 18 and 49 use social media. Facebook still has more followers than Instagram. Cross-posting is a quick way to reach most of the adults in the school community. Pew researchers found that the highest number of adult users of a social media platform use YouTube. Given the variety of video-based platforms, learners have tended to gravitate to TikTok. This platform also seems to be attracting more adults—21 percent, according to the 2021 Pew *Social Media Fact Sheet*. The Pew *Teens, Social Media and Technology 2022* report (Vogels, Gelles-Watnick, and Massarat 2022) shows that most teens have dropped Facebook in favor of TikTok, Instagram, and Snapchat (figure 8.1). And 95 percent of teens use YouTube—school libraries need to be there to reach both learners and adults. We need to become influencers for our brand!

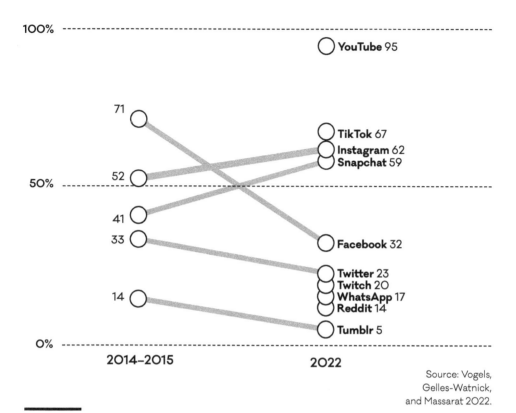

FIGURE 8.1

Teen use of social media platforms

Note: "Teen" refers to those ages 13–17. Those who did not give an answer are not shown. The 2014–15 survey did not ask about YouTube, Twitch, WhatsApp, and Reddit. TikTok debuted globally in 2018.

Continuous Feedback, Evaluation, and Sustainability

In order to maintain brand integrity and accountability, establishing feedback loops to evaluate users' experience with your services and resources is a critical prong in building a sustainable school library brand. Consider how you can leverage some of the following strategies in your communications plan to gather input and engage your various audiences:

- *User surveys:* Include Likert scale and open-ended response questions to determine whether messaging is understood, whether audience needs have been addressed, and whether there are emerging needs that must be considered.
- *Moderator managed online feedback:* Provide an opportunity on your school library website for the target audience to share their likes/dislikes and ideas regarding school libraries. Include a disclaimer noting that all comments are

reviewed for compliance with school and district digital citizenship expectations before they are approved for posting.

- *Social media accounts:* Use your school library accounts to not only post about news, upcoming events, services and resources, and the like, but also to take advantage of the opportunity to respond to comments, answer questions, and address complaints or misunderstandings. Gather and examine the data related to comments, shares, or likes as a valuable feedback loop for brand building.
- *Focus groups and interviews:* Assess effectiveness of instruction, events, and services.
- *Library advisory committee:* Establish your school-based library advisory committee to ensure ongoing dialogue with and among stakeholders regarding brand growth and image as well as provide input related to policies and procedures.
- *Instructional and usage data:* Review data sources regularly to determine patterns, identify gaps, and make informed decisions for improvement.

Return on Investment

There are costs related to effective communications in terms of time spent, production, printing, postage, artwork, and more, but there is also a demonstrable return on investment when done well. Although you may cringe at the thought of having to allocate a portion of an already limited budget to communications, increased funds are often the result when your school library brand creates a buzz with target audiences and an acknowledgment of the importance of the school library in the lives of all learners.

We hope we have conveyed the importance of the "why" of creating and implementing a communications plan for the success of the school library brand. Think about it. You've spent all this time working on evaluating your program and tweaking your user experience, refining your look and your messaging, and overcoming your brand barriers. You must make the investment—time, effort, funds—in good communications so that your users can benefit. It is the culminating step! And the return on your investment is an informed and fulfilled learning community.

Questions for the Reflective Practitioner

1 If you do not have a school library supervisor, which administrator, or group of librarians, can you connect with to develop a communications plan for your school library?

2 What messaging is most important to your learning community?

3 Which of the traditional communication vehicles would be most effective to promote your brand?

4 How might you ramp up your school library social media presence to reach more stake-holders?

CONCLUSION

Give me a place to stand, and a lever long enough, and I will move the world.

—Archimedes ([287–212 BCE] 1957)

We began with the basic premise that this book was *not* going to be about creating a personal brand, tagline, or logo—rather, it would be about embracing and developing a brand for the school library and the school librarian. We argued that "perception is everything" and provided evidence that the perception of school libraries is often associated with unpleasant experiences and related emotions, rules that are slanted in favor of the librarian and "their" library, and an overall lack of recognition that the landscape is ever evolving and that we must evolve, too. Unless we align our actions with legendary brand behavior to engender loyalty and a strong base of support, we fear that the school library profession may be looking at an extinction-level event. However, we remain hopeful because we are constantly inspired by people in our profession who have helped move us forward and changed our world. Through the auspices of our national and state associations, many thoughtful, reflective professionals share their stories, best practices, and research to lead us along new pathways to excellence. The *National School Library Standards* reflect the collective wisdom of legions of workaday school librarians who may never be recognized as rock stars among us, but on their home turf, they are living legends because they deliver what their learning communities care about and need.

As we considered lessons from the business world, the use of personas emerged as a way to help amplify and acknowledge that user wants and needs are not static but dynamic and must be examined regularly. User-centered design allows us to be intentional and to engage on a more meaningful and focused level.

Throughout, we have emphasized that "school libraries are dynamic learning environments that bridge the gap between [equitable] access and opportunity for all learners" (AASL 2018a, 1). We must listen to our users, empathize with them, provide resources, services, and instruction that they don't even know they need—yet. Any design we develop for our school library must be centered on the user, constantly evaluated, and our practices and services must change as our stakeholders' needs evolve.

Additionally, we explored the development of "service culture." This concept is invaluable in creating positive relationships and a baseline consistency of user experience. Remember—what would Nordstrom do? For us, the AASL Standards provide agreed-upon indicators of what can be reliably expected of our brand. As we looked at examples of how various libraries have grown the library brand to be more inclusive of the ever-changing interests of their communities, their common thread and main objective came through loud and clear: making memories that engender loyalty.

Our survey of practitioners regarding school library brand versus personal brand validated that standards-based consistency of experience in pre-service preparation and professional practice is essential. Our respondents clearly considered AASL Standards and the specific culture and needs of the learning community they serve. This was a key to their success. They exemplified the stickiness factor because sustainability is ensured when you are focused on the school library brand more than your own.

We also took time to examine the value of observation and use of data to inform our actions in elevating the brand. Both are important tools to leverage in identifying demand-driven wants and in forecasting emerging trends. Observation, data, and evaluation provide us with an increased understanding of our audiences and assist us in developing action agendas that are in sync with evidence.

Identifying and sussing out the barriers to positive brand development was uncomfortable but necessary for understanding all the variables that any school librarian may encounter. Nonetheless, our excursion to Gaver City allowed us the opportunity to observe and learn as various personas from the *National School Library Standards* faced the obstacles as a team, using positive energy, knowledge of their learning community, research, data, evidence, and the AASL Standards to resolve them.

Our ongoing emphasis on communications has been more than deliberate. It has been designed as a wake-up call to anyone who has yet to realize that communication is the coin of the realm. It must be conscious, continuous, and carefully constructed to convey key messages. It must also be a two-way conversation with each identified target audience to facilitate an exchange of ideas and information that will ensure the ongoing maintenance and sustainability of the school library brand.

We hope that reading this book has provided you a better understanding of how important it is to assess your own situation by considering what we have covered, and how, by promoting the school library in alignment with the AASL Standards, you will gain credibility, and the school library will be a valued brand. Most importantly, you *can* change your world. Seriously. By the world, we mean change that impacts your learners, your educators, your community. We have every confidence that you have been doing your best, but as the great Maya Angelou is often attributed to have said, "Do the best you can until you know better. Then when you know better, do better." We can all do better—we'll join you on the journey!

APPENDIX A
School Library Branding Persona Template

Using the data you have collected about and from your learning community, develop three to five personas that represent groups of your school library stakeholders as a step in the development of your school library brand. This template (shown on the following page) can be adapted to depict learners, other educators, staff, administrators, parents, and community members.

The *School Library Branding Persona Template* is also available as a Google Form (https://tinyurl.com/55f5u4bs) and was adapted from the following sources:

Creative Companion. n.d. "Persona Core Poster." creativecompanion.files.wordpress
.com/2011/05/persona-core-poster_creative-companion1.pdf.

McCready, Ryan. 2021. "20+ User Persona Examples, Templates and Tips for Targeted
Decision-Making." Venngage. September 22, 2021. venngage.com/blog/user
-persona-examples/.

Usability.gov. n.d. "Persona Development Discussion Guide." usability.gov/how-to-and
-tools/resources/templates/persona-development-discussion-guide.html.

Persona Profile

SCENARIO
How would this persona benefit from using the school library?

Name: (Not the name of an actual person)

Role: (Profession/title, learner, etc.)

DEMOGRAPHICS
Gender Identity: (How does this persona identify themselves?)

Age Group: (Age, grade level, years teaching [early career, midcareer, late career], years of experience in job)

Ethnicity: (Cultural and racial identity)

Educational Background: (Highest year of formal education and/or degree earned)

Other Demographics That Matter to Your Library: (Income levels, head of household variables, English as a new language, etc.)

PERSONALITY
Is this persona outgoing and friendly; shy and reserved; introverted or extroverted; judgmental?

PASSIONS
What interests this persona? Consider hobbies/clubs, beliefs, activities, and so on.

Quote: Express what is important to this persona with a quote. Does it relate to your library?

PRIORITIES/GOALS
What drives this persona and what do they hope to achieve?

FAVORITE BOOKS

Book Title
By Author Name

Book Title
By Author Name

Book Title
By Author Name

TECHNOLOGY LEVEL
How does this persona use and integrate technology in their daily lives?

LEARNING VARIABILITY
What physical, emotional, or intellectual challenges are faced by this persona?

FRUSTRATIONS
What keeps this persona up at night?

MOTIVATIONS
What is most important to this persona and their purpose in life?

APPENDIX B
Checklist for School Libraries

In our Gaver City school scenario in chapter 7, library supervisor Margot and the district librarians expanded and customized the School Library Evaluation Checklist from the *National School Library Standards* (AASL 2018b, 174–180). Using an evaluation tool to take the pulse of the school libraries in their district was a critical first step to identifying brand barriers and setting healthy goals to rebrand school libraries across the district.

The checklist and evaluation tool that follows was built, adapted, and updated based on the decades-long evolution of school library standards. A Likert scale was designed to help assess the current strengths and weaknesses of the school library. Section 7 of the evaluation addresses district leadership over the school library program. The concepts in this section should be rated even if no supervisor/director position exists—or if a distributed leadership approach is in place—because it is important to know whether these needs are being addressed.

The school library evaluation process should involve as many people from the learning community as possible to fully assess the well-being of the school library brand, create buy-in, and build advocates. Precisely who should be involved at each point in the process, how long the process should take, what components must be addressed, and the nature of the plans developed through the process will vary with each school.

Areas Included

1. School Library Program
2. School Librarian Roles and Responsibilities
3. Leadership, Planning, and Management (building-level)
4. Personnel
5. Resources and Equipment
6. Facilities and Flexible Learning Environments
7. District Leadership

School Library Program

O = Nonexistent, 1 = Poor, 2 = Fair, 3 = Good, 4 = Excellent, N/A = Not applicable

		O	1	2	3	4	N/A
1.1	The school library plays a critical role in teaching and learning activities.						
1.2	The school library is fully integrated into the curriculum, serving the school's educational goals and objectives by providing access to information and ideas and technology for the entire school community.						
1.3	The principal, the school librarian, other educators, and learners work together to ensure that the school library contributes fully to the educational process in the school.						
1.4	The school library offers both traditional resources and innovative technologies as teaching and learning tools.						
1.5	The school library maintains a physical, virtual, and social media presence.						
1.6	The school library is housed in facilities that provide adequate and appropriate space for all the resources and activities.						
1.7	School library facilities are convenient, comfortable, and aesthetically inviting.						

The School Librarian: Roles and Responsibilities

O = Nonexistent, 1 = Poor, 2 = Fair, 3 = Good, 4 = Excellent, N/A = Not applicable

Information Specialist/Digital Learning Specialist		O	1	2	3	4	N/A
2.1	In accordance with district policy, develop and maintain a collection of resources appropriate to the curriculum, the learners, and the teaching styles and instructional strategies used within the school community.						
2.2	Make resources available to learners through a systematically developed and organized collection within the school and cooperate and network with other libraries, librarians, and agencies to provide access to resources outside the school for maximum and effective use.						
2.3	Provide access to the collection via an accurate and efficient retrieval system that uses the expanded searching capabilities of digital tools.						

Information Specialist/Digital Learning Specialist *(cont'd)*		O	1	2	3	4	N/A
2.4	Model and develop a commitment to respect equity, diversity, and inclusion in collection development and within the learning community.						
2.5	Empower all members of the learning community to become critical thinkers, enthusiastic readers, skillful researchers, curators, and ethical users of information.						
2.6	Support learners' success by guiding them to read for understanding, breadth, and pleasure.						
2.7	Provide all learners with assistance in identifying, locating, and interpreting information resources.						
2.8	Support learners as they make meaning for themselves to create new knowledge by collecting, organizing, and sharing resources of personal relevance.						
2.9	Ensure that all learners have access to the school library and to qualified professional staff throughout the school day. Class visits are scheduled flexibly to encourage use at point of need.						
2.10	Circulation policies and procedures ensure that access to information is not impeded by fees, loan restrictions, or other barriers.						
2.11	Other educators, student learners, parents, and administrators are regularly informed of new material, equipment, and services that meet their information and learning needs.						
2.12	Learners at remote sites are provided access to information.						
2.13	Evaluate, promote, and use existing and emerging technologies to support teaching and learning.						
2.14	Champion equity, access, and intellectual freedom for users within the physical space and beyond, including providing 24/7 access to the online library, to digital and audio books, and to various information resources and tech integration services.						
2.15	Provide guidance in the evaluation of resources (including digital resources and services and technology) and develop processes for such evaluation.						
2.16	Understand, model, and champion copyright, fair use, licensing of intellectual property, privacy concerns related to use of digital resources and the Internet, and ethical online behavior, and assist users with their understanding and observance of the same.						

Teacher		O	1	2	3	4	N/A
2.17	Teach information and technology literacy as an integral part of the content and objectives of the school's curriculum.						
2.18	Provide instruction in accessing, selecting, evaluating, and communicating information and in the production of media.						
2.19	Collaborate and co-teach with classroom educators to establish learning objectives and assessment strategies to develop individual and group inquiry-based learning experiences.						
2.20	Collaborate with classroom or content-area educators and specialists to plan, deliver, and evaluate instruction in information and technology literacy for all learners.						
2.21	Provide assistance in the use of technology to access information outside the school.						
2.22	Provide other educators and staff learning opportunities related to new technologies, use and production of a variety of media, and laws and policies regarding information.						
2.23	Use a variety of instructional methods with different user groups and encourage personal creativity and innovation.						
2.24	Empower learners to work with each other in successful collaborations and to constructively assess their own work and the work of their peers.						
2.25	Foster exploration, discovery, creation, and innovation in a growth mindset.						
2.26	Teach all members of the learning community to engage with and use information in a global society.						

Instructional Partner		O	1	2	3	4	N/A
2.27	Participate in the curriculum development process at both the building and district levels to ensure that the curricula include the full range of literacy skills (information, media, visual, digital, data, social, and technological) necessary to meet content standards and to develop lifelong learners.						
2.28	Offer other educators assistance in using information and technology resources, acquiring/assessing materials, and incorporating information and technology literacy skills into curriculum.						

Instructional Partner *(cont'd)*		0	1	2	3	4		N/A
2.29	Collaborate with other educators to design and deliver engaging inquiry-based learning experiences as well as assessments that incorporate multiple literacies and foster critical thinking.							
2.30	Participate in the implementation of collaboratively planned learning experiences by providing group and individual instruction, assessing learner progress, and evaluating activities.							
2.31	Use a systematic instructional development and information search process in collaborating with other educators to improve integration of learning technology into curriculum.							
2.32	Provide leadership in the assessment, evaluation, and implementation of information and instructional technologies.							
2.33	Plan and provide professional development opportunities within the school and district for and with all staff, including other school librarians.							

Administrator		0	1	2	3	4		N/A
2.34	Work collaboratively with members of the learning community to define the policies of the school library and guide and direct activities related to it.							
2.35	Maximize the efficiency and effectiveness of the school library by using strategic planning for continuous improvement.							
2.36	Ensure that school library goals and objectives are aligned with school and district long-range strategic plans.							
2.37	Use effective management principles, including the supervision of personnel, resources, and facilities, in developing and implementing school library goals and objectives.							
2.38	Conduct ongoing action research and evaluation that creates data used to inform continuous school library improvement.							
2.39	Use evidence of effective practice, particularly in terms of learning outcomes, to demonstrate relevance and support school library goals and planning.							

(continued)

Administrator *(cont'd)*		O	1	2	3	4	N/A
2.40	Supervise and evaluate support staff, which may include educational assistants, volunteers, and student assistants.						
2.41	Prepare, justify, and administer the school library budget to support specific goals.						
2.42	Establish processes and procedures for selection, acquisition, circulation, resource sharing, and the like to ensure that resources are available when needed.						
2.43	Create and maintain a teaching and learning environment that is inviting, safe, flexible, and conducive to student learning.						
2.44	Select and use effective tech applications for management purposes.						
2.45	Participate in the recruiting, hiring, and training of other professionals, educational assistants, learners, and volunteer staff.						
2.46	Arrange for flexible scheduling of the facilities to provide learner accessibility to staff and resources at point of need.						
2.47	Ensure equitable physical access to facilities by providing barrier-free, universally designed environments.						

Leader		O	1	2	3	4	N/A
2.48	Develop and support the school's and the school library's mission, strategic plan, and policies.						
2.49	Serve on decision-making teams in the school and participate in school improvement and accreditation activities.						
2.50	Create an environment that is conducive to active and participatory learning, resource-based instructional practices, and collaboration with teaching staff.						
2.51	Share with the learning community collaboratively developed and up-to-date district policies concerning such issues as materials selection, circulation, reconsideration of materials, copyright, privacy, and responsible use of technology and social media.						
2.52	Evaluate, introduce, and model emerging technologies for the learning community and use technology to supplement school resources.						

Leader *(cont'd)*		O	1	2	3	4	N/A
2.53	Encourage the use of instructional technology to engage learners and to improve learning, providing 24/7 access to digital information resources for the entire learning community.						
2.54	Collect and analyze data to improve instruction and to demonstrate correlations between the school library and student achievement.						
2.55	Maintain active memberships in professional associations.						
2.56	Remain current in professional practices and developments, information technologies, and education research applicable to the school library.						
2.57	Address broader educational issues with other educators in the building, at the district level, and at the professional association level.						
2.58	Participate as an active leader of the local and global learning community, building relationships with stakeholders.						
2.59	Maintain frequent and timely communication to stakeholders through the school and library website, parent newsletter, e-mail, social media, and other formats, such as local cable access television, video/audio streaming, and on-demand videos and podcasts.						
2.60	Use local, state, national, and international school library data and research to engage support.						
2.61	Submit regular reports providing evidence of what the school library and school librarian do to prepare learners to be successful.						
2.62	Demonstrate a commitment to maintaining intellectual freedom.						
2.63	Promote the ethical use of information.						
2.64	Create an environment in which collaboration, innovation, and creative problem-solving thrive.						
2.65	Welcome and encourage input to create consensus.						
2.66	Share expertise by presenting at faculty meetings, parent meetings, and school board meetings.						

Leadership, Planning, and Management

O = Nonexistent, 1 = Poor, 2 = Fair, 3 = Good, 4 = Excellent, N/A = Not applicable

		O	1	2	3	4	N/A
3.1	The mission, goals, and objectives of the school library are clearly understood and fully supported by the administration and educational staff, the students, and the community.						
3.2	Responsibility for leading and managing the school library is shared equally by the school librarian, the principal, and a district-level supervisor or director, who must jointly develop goals, establish priorities, and allocate the resources necessary to accomplish the mission.						
3.3	Planning involves district program administrators, school library staff, school administrators, other educators, student learners, and community members, as appropriate.						
3.4	As part of the planning process, the school library is evaluated regularly to review overall goals and objectives in relation to user and instructional needs and to assess the efficiency and effectiveness of specific activities.						
3.5	School library and personnel evaluations follow district-wide policies and procedures, focus on performance, and are based upon appropriate collected data and evidence.						
3.6	The planning process results in periodic reports that emphasize and document progress toward stated goals and objectives.						
3.7	The school librarian, the principal, and the district-level supervisor or director cooperatively plan the budget.						
3.8	Sufficient funds are provided for the resources and personnel necessary to achieve the goals and objectives of the school library.						
3.9	The quality and size of the professional and support staff are directly related to the range and level of services provided.						
3.10	The selection, training, support, and evaluation of the staff are valued as key determinants in the success of the school library.						
3.11	The school library is promoted by school library personnel who demonstrate the importance of the school library in education, publicize available services and resources to all learners, serve on school and district-wide committees, and participate in community-wide projects.						

Personnel

O = Nonexistent, 1 = Poor, 2 = Fair, 3 = Good, 4 = Excellent, N/A = Not applicable

		O	1	2	3	4	N/A
4.1	Each school, regardless of size or level, has at least one full-time certified school librarian.						
4.2	The number of professional staff in the school building is determined through an identified planning process that considers school library requirements, the number of student learners and classroom educators who are served, and other pertinent features of the school library.						
4.3	School librarians are members of the school's instructional staff and participate fully in the planning, delivery, and evaluation of the school curriculum and of student learning activities.						
4.4	School librarians have master's-level education or equivalent, with preparation in library and information science, management, education, media, communications theory, and technology.						
4.5	One or more paid technician, assistant, or clerk is provided for each professional school librarian.						
4.6	School library personnel are available throughout the school day and do not have their time rigidly scheduled with classes.						
4.7	School librarians are evaluated with instruments that address their unique responsibilities and contributions according to established district practices for all professional personnel.						
4.8	School library staff members have salary, fringe benefits, and working conditions equal to those of other staff members with comparable qualifications and responsibilities.						
4.9	School librarians are accorded pay, responsibilities, and standing commensurate with other leadership positions in the school.						
4.10	School librarians engage in continuing education activities to ensure that they are qualified to manage and lead school libraries that reflect the most recent developments in education, technology, and information science.						
4.11	Leadership and coordination are provided at the district level by a supervisor/director chosen on the basis of education preparation, breadth of experience, and administrative qualifications.						

Resources and Equipment

O = Nonexistent, 1 = Poor, 2 = Fair, 3 = Good, 4 = Excellent, N/A = Not applicable

Scope of the Collection		O	1	2	3	4	N/A
5.1	The school library collection is selected/developed by the school librarian and faculty to support curriculum and contribute to teaching and learning.						
5.2	The collection includes resources in a variety of formats with appropriate equipment and technology selected to meet the learning needs of all student learners.						
5.3	Resources are provided from outside the school through interlibrary/agency loan and other means to extend/expand the collection.						

Collection Development		O	1	2	3	4	N/A
5.4	A collection-development policy is in place, and approved by the school board, which includes criteria/procedures for selection/reconsideration.						
5.5	Each school has its own collection-development plan that supplements district policy and provides specific guidelines for developing the school's collection.						
5.6	Resources are selected according to principles of intellectual freedom and provide all learners access to information that represents diverse points of view in a pluralistic society.						

Organization, Maintenance. and Circulation		O	1	2	3	4	N/A
5.7	Materials are included in a local bibliographic control system, and standardized formats for classification and cataloging are followed.						
5.8	Automation of library circulation, cataloging, and acquisition is in place.						
5.9	Collections and equipment are circulated/accessed according to procedures that ensure confidentiality of records and promote access.						

Information Access beyond the School	O	1	2	3	4	N/A
5.10 The building-level school library participates in interlibrary/agency loans, as a lender as well as a borrower, according to established policies and procedures.						
5.11 The school library maintains a vibrant web presence that provides access to a wide variety of digital and other electronic resources that have been carefully created or selected and vetted according to the district and school collection development policy.						

Facilities and Flexible Learning Environments

O = Nonexistent, 1 = Poor, 2 = Fair, 3 = Good, 4 = Excellent, N/A = Not applicable

School Building Facilities	O	1	2	3	4	N/A
6.1 Facilities and flexible learning environments (FLEs) are barrier-free and provide unimpeded physical or virtual access for users.						
6.2 Facilities/FLEs have fluid design, so that changing needs and newer information-handling technologies can be accommodated in the existing complex or delivery platform without extensive redesign.						
6.3 Facilities/FLEs are located and designed to provide easy access and encourage frequent use, allowing for traffic flow that minimizes interruptions and distractions.						
6.4 Facilities (physical) have a separate outside entrance and are located to make them readily accessible before, during, and after school hours and during vacation periods.						
6.5 Facilities/FLEs provide a comfortable, efficient, and safe working environment for student learners, other educators, administrators, and school library staff.						
6.6 Facilities (physical) include adequate space for independent study, small- and large-group activities, reference service, manual and electronic access to the collection, circulation activities, and informal or recreational reading.						

(continued)

School Building Facilities *(cont'd)*		O	1	2	3	4	N/A
6.7	Facilities (physical) have sufficient space to conduct the support functions (administrative, technical, and consultant) required in providing instruction, materials, and services.						
6.8	Facilities (physical) have sufficient space for housing materials and the equipment required for production, for evaluation activities, and for the use of such materials and equipment.						
6.9	Facilities/FLEs are functional in design and arrangement, aesthetically pleasing in appearance, and convenient and comfortable to use.						
6.10	Facilities (physical) have the requisite natural and artificial lighting, acoustical treatment, and climate control for the comfort of the user and for the preservation of materials and equipment.						
6.11	Facilities (physical) are designed to provide the necessary electrical power, light control, circuit surge, telephone and intercommunication devices, sound control, lighting protection, and electronic capabilities required to meet the needs of a changing technological environment.						
6.12	Facilities (physical) are designed with attention to safety precautions such as fire preparedness, emergency exits, securely fastened equipment, and other safeguards that will minimize risk to learners, faculty, and staff.						
6.13	Facilities (physical) provide for the unobtrusive security of materials and equipment during the school day and utilize additional electronic and other security measures during nonuse hours.						
6.14	The size of the overall school library and its spaces, and the relationship of those spaces to each other, helps determine the number of library staff needed to manage and supervise the center.						

District Library Facilities		O	1	2	3	4	N/A
6.15	Functions and services are planned in relation to district goals and building-level programs.						
6.16	Personnel assigned to district library facilities have adequate working space, sufficient equipment, and a pleasing environment.						

District Leadership

O = Nonexistent, 1 = Poor, 2 = Fair, 3 = Good, 4 = Excellent, N/A = Not applicable

A district supervisor or director performs the following essential functions:

Leadership		O	1	2	3	4	N/A
7.1	Develops an effective plan and process for providing school libraries that support the philosophy, goals, and objectives of the school district.						
7.2	Provides leadership and guidance to the school library staff in school library planning, curriculum development, budgeting, in-service activities, facility use, and production.						
7.3	Participates in curriculum development, facility planning, personnel staffing, budget and management committees, and task forces and teams at the administrative level.						
7.4	Articulates a code of ethics that promotes adherence to policies and guidelines for honoring copyright, intellectual property, privacy, and the responsible use of the Internet.						
7.5	Advocates the principles of intellectual freedom that govern the universal right to read and to access information and ideas.						
7.6	Provides leadership in evaluating the impact of new and existing technologies and program features, and encourages use of the most effective technologies and strategies to support teaching and learning.						
7.7	Directs the district's participation in library/agency networking.						
7.8	Fosters development of exemplary school libraries at each educational level, and assists the school libraries in meeting regional, state, and national standards.						
7.9	Provides district in-service activities for school librarians to encourage leadership, competence, and creativity in developing school libraries.						
7.10	Assists principals, school librarians, and others in applying district policies that relate to school libraries.						
7.11	Plays a leading role in the district technology committee that has responsibility for the ongoing review and updating of a multiyear technology plan for school board and state approval.						
7.12	Participates actively in state and national professional associations, and encourages a high level of participation by other school library personnel at the district and building levels.						

Consultation		O	1	2	3	4		N/A
7.13	Assists school librarians in developing school library goals and objectives.							
7.14	Promotes expansion of programs that integrate the teaching of information and technology literacy with the teaching of subject content.							
7.15	Demonstrates methods for effective integration of school library activities and instructional units in building-level school libraries.							
7.16	Consults with planning committees and architects when new or remodeled facilities are designed.							

Communication		O	1	2	3	4		N/A
7.17	Advises district and school administrators about new developments in school library practice, media for learning, technology, instructional strategies, and research.							
7.18	Conducts orientation meetings about the school library for other educators, administrators, and support staff.							
7.19	Develops—or finds—and then implements plans for presenting and publicizing programs and services and for communicating goals and priorities to the staff and public.							
7.20	Prepares reports for district and school administrators on the impact of building-level school libraries on the instructional process and success.							
7.21	Submits reports to the school board, state and national agencies, school library and technology integration staff, and the public.							

Coordination		O	1	2	3	4		N/A
7.22	Designs and supervises implementation of a learning technology curriculum (in coordination with district- and building-level instructional leaders and school librarians).							
7.23	Participates in curriculum development and implementation through membership on instructional, curriculum, textbook, technology, professional development, and new program adoption committees.							

Coordination *(cont'd)*	O	1	2	3	4	N/A
7.24 Coordinates the planning and development of K–12 school libraries that serve the learners and staff within the schools.						
7.25 Coordinates the acquisition and circulation of as well as access to specialized collections that enrich the curriculum for all grade levels.						
7.26 Guides school librarians in selection of materials and equipment to ensure unified ordering and economies of scale for periodicals, supplies, and equipment for all schools in the district.						
7.27 Investigates and negotiates district-wide licensing of products and services.						
7.28 Ensures standardization of technical services (circulation, classification, cataloging, processing, standard nomenclature, naming conventions, etc.).						

Administration	O	1	2	3	4	N/A
7.29 Works with principals to recruit, supervise, and evaluate school librarians and technology integration personnel.						
7.30 Works with principals to ensure that the school libraries further the teaching and learning process.						
7.31 Assists school librarians and principals in developing building-level budgets.						
7.32 Develops the district budget, including any allocation for each school, in cooperation with principals and school librarians.						
7.33 Interprets school library and related budget needs for appropriate administrators.						
7.34 Monitors state and federal laws pertaining to school library and technology integration programs.						
7.35 Monitors collections, services, and equipment to provide data on use, relevance, and currency.						
7.36 Arranges for school librarians to evaluate new resources, services, and equipment.						
7.37 Negotiates contracts and supervises purchase and installation of resources.						

(continued)

Administration *(cont'd)*		O	1	2	3	4	N/A
7.38	Manages technical services for acquiring and processing resources and for maintaining and circulating district-owned materials and equipment.						
7.39	Monitors and publicizes the status of district compliance with regional, state, and national accreditation requirements and library and technology standards.						
7.40	Seeks and administers grants from federal, state, and local agencies and foundations.						
7.41	Monitors instruction and training for implementation of technology initiatives.						
7.42	Evaluates the impact of school libraries at the district and building levels.						

Source: Susan D. Ballard (2022), *A Checklist for School Libraries*, an unpublished manuscript updated and adapted using the following:

AASL. 2007. *Standards for the 21st-Century Learner*. Chicago: AASL.

———. 2009. *Empowering Learners: Guidelines for School Library Programs*. Chicago: AASL.

———. 2010. *Learning4Life Sample Job Description: School Librarian*.

———. 2018. *National School Library Standards for Learners, School Librarians, and School Libraries*. Chicago: ALA Editions.

———. 2020. *School Librarian Job Description*. standards.aasl.org/wp-content/uploads/2020/04/SL-Job-Description_3-30-2020.pdf.

Meyers, J. K. 1988. *Information Power: Checklist for School Library Media Programs*. Chicago: American Association of School Librarians and Association for Educational Communications and Technology.

APPENDIX C
Budget Summary Framework

Name of School

Vision of the School Library
Include your vision, which is an aspirational statement to help stakeholders understand where the school library brand is heading. For example: It is our vision that the school library will provide a safe, welcoming, and user-centered environment that offers all learners equitable and responsive access to up-to-date and well-managed resources and technology to meet their academic and personal needs. The school library will foster an appreciation of reading and ensure opportunities for all learners to see themselves reflected in literature as well as provide for the seamless integration of technology into educational and work settings.

Mission of the School Library
Include a mission statement (aligned with the school mission and the district mission) that helps distinguish the school library as a unique brand. For example: The mission of the school library is to prepare learners for life in an information-rich society through the provision of thoughtfully selected resources and instruction on how to access information efficiently and to critically assess resources through classroom and personalized instructional experiences.

Description of the School Library
Populate this section with information about the major services and responsibilities of the school library, such as the following: • Lifelong appreciation of learning promoted through reading, viewing, and listening. • Intellectual and physical access to the school library and technology resources. • Information literacy, research, and technology skills, developed through assured learning experiences. • Individual instruction and guidance in the use of materials, including emerging technologies and online and electronic resources and research assistance. • Collaboration with other educators to plan, develop, implement, and evaluate instructional units. • Shared responsibility for the integration of information literacy skills, research, and technology skills within the curriculum. • Selection of materials and resources to align with curriculum objectives. • Training of faculty and staff in the effective use of resources and technology. • Coordination and distribution of equipment. • Partnership with school administrators to effectively articulate and implement school library goals and objectives.

Goals, Objectives, and Activities
In general, goals, objectives, and activities involve four areas of effort: • Curriculum Instruction and Assessment • Professional Development • Communications • Operations
Major Budget Assumptions
Discuss the development of the school library budget as it relates to the following: • The achievement of school district educational goals and school board policies • State, accreditation, and national guidelines and standards • Budget history • Enrollment • Documentation of need
Priorities
Describe the most pressing needs of the school library and how each helps develop the brand and achieve results.
Critical Success Factors and Performance Indicators
Provide a summary of evidence showing that the investment in the school library brand has delivered results and has resulted in growth. Discuss how the school library has contributed to district goals for student learning as expressed in local graduation standards and benchmarks for all subject areas through the infusion of information literacy and technology within the curriculum. In addition, provide other performance indicators such as data related to collection development/mapping, circulation, inventory, and usage records (e.g., level of collaboration rubrics, class and individual visits to the library, stakeholder surveys).

APPENDIX D
Recommended Reading

Chapter 1: Brand or Brand Behavior?

Coatney, Sharon, and Violet H. Harada, eds. 2017. *The Many Faces of School Library Leadership*. 2nd ed. Santa Barbara, CA: Libraries Unlimited.

> The many "faces" in this second edition of Coatney and Harada's excellent resource are some of the greatest leaders in our profession, who share their invaluable insights on school library leadership. The essays offer opportunities for reflection on personal leadership, and thus brand behavior, for advocacy, intellectual freedom, literacy, technology, and leadership styles that can improve effective leadership and brand, making a difference for learners as well as for your brand as a leader.

Martin, Ann M., and Kathleen Riopelle Roberts. 2019. *Leadership: Strategic Thinking, Decision Making, Communication, and Relationship Building*. Chicago: AASL.

> Martin and Roberts connect the *National School Library Standards* to the leadership role of school librarians, examining strategic thinking, decision making, communication, relationship building, and the connection to leadership styles and skills—making a difference for learner growth. Each section includes reflective questions, self-assessment tools, and breakthrough skills, giving school librarians a solid foundation for leadership growth. The authors offer strategies and tools to elevate practices, and, though not explicitly mentioned, brand behavior is an aspect of leadership for school librarians at every level of experience.

Moreillon, Judi. 2018. *Maximizing School Librarian Leadership*. Chicago: ALA.

> Embracing and enhancing the leadership role of librarians in a school setting results in school librarians making a strong impact on student learning through collaboration with educators, administrators, and the school community. Moreillon offers inspiration and support for improving perceptions of school librarians (i.e., brand behavior) as crucial educators for student learning—with ALA Web Extras!

Pallotta, Dan. 2011. "A Logo Is Not a Brand." *Harvard Business Review*. Last modified June 15, 2011. hbr.org/2011/06/a-logo-is-not-a-brand.

> An experienced, nonprofit sector innovator details what brand is. This definition includes strategy, call to action, customer service, the way you speak,

communication tools, your people, your facilities, and, yes, logo and visuals, though the latter are not the most crucial elements for the school library brand.

Chapter 2: Lessons from the Business World (User-Centered Design)

Dam, Rikke Friis, and Teo Yu Siang. n.d. "Empathy Map—Why and How to Use It." Interaction Design Foundation. interaction-design.org/literature/article/empathy-map-why-and-how-to-use-it.

> The authors provide good guiding questions to help develop insights about learners' needs.

Deisley, Laura. 2016. "Bringing Design Thinking to the School Library." Edutopia. October 4, 2016. edutopia.org/article/bringing-design-thinking-to-the-school-library-laura-deisley.

> Deisley suggests seven practical steps for using design thinking to uncover unmet needs and develop innovative new practices in school libraries.

IDEO U. 2022. "Design Thinking Resources." IDEO U. Last modified 2022. ideou.com/pages/design-thinking-resources.

> This is the mothership of design thinking resources. It includes links to activities, frameworks, courses, case studies, articles, and toolkits. Especially useful is the *Design Thinking for Educators Toolkit* (ideo.com/post/design-thinking-for-educators), which contains the process and methods for design along with the *Designer's Workbook*, adapted specifically for the context of K–12 education.

Interaction Design Foundation. n.d. *The Basics of User Experience Design.* interaction-design.org/ebook.

> For an introduction into the world of user experience (UX) design or a refresher, this free, downloadable UX design book covers many of the important topics in the field—topics that can be applied effectively by school librarians, such as interaction design (the psychology of motion and feedback), design thinking (an iterative, empathy-based problem-solving process), and usability (how easily a product or a service can be used).

Chapter 3: Development of a Service Culture

"Nordstrom Opens a NYC Flagship Store." 2019. Video. YouTube. Posted by CBS Sunday Morning, December 15, 2019. youtube.com/watch?v=XCcPiXlTeZo.

> A *CBS Sunday Morning* report on why, when other retail stores were shutting their doors, the Nordstrom family decided to open their first New York City store. Did they think NYC needed another department store? No. NYC needed Nordstrom! Viewing this short video will help you understand the making and maintaining of a service culture.

Spector, Robert, and breAnne O. Reeves. 2017. *The Nordstrom Way to Customer Service Excellence: Creating a Values-Driven Service Culture.* 3rd ed. Hoboken, NJ: John Wiley & Sons.

> Updated edition of *The Nordstrom Way* that focuses not so much on strategies and practices but on nine nonnegotiable core values that define the Nordstrom culture. These values serve as the foundation for creating a culture of innovation and adaptation that ensures that the brand remains relevant.

Chapter 4: School Library Brand versus Personal Brand

Johnson, Mica. 2018. "Personal Branding to Promote School Librarians." *Knowledge Quest.* February 23, 2018. knowledgequest.aasl.org/personal-branding-promote-school-librarians.

> This *Knowledge Quest* blog post does an excellent job of explaining how a personal brand should be used to promote the school library and school librarian brand versus one's own interests.

Weisburg, Hilda K. 2023. *Leading for School Librarians: There Is No Other Option.* 2nd ed. Chicago: Neal-Schuman.

> Chapter 9, "Always Have a Plan," includes an excellent take on the concept of brand for the school library. A key idea to remember is that "you need to identify your brand and create taglines to aid your planning and promote your library program."

Chapter 5: Observation, Data, and Action

Andrews, Sandra D. 2012. *The Power of Data: An Introduction to Using National Data to Support School Library Programs.* Chicago: AASL.

> Though a bit dated, this is a good primer on the use of datasets to establish goals for the school library. The author also considers how to use data effectively to advocate for school libraries with a variety of stakeholder groups and thus imprint brand identity and value.

Ballard, Susan D. 2017. "Diving Lessons: Taking the Data Literacy Plunge through Action Research." In *Creating Data Literate Students*, edited by Kristin Fontichiaro, Jo Angela Oehrli, and Amy Lennex, 305–38. Ann Arbor, MI: Maize Books/Michigan Publishing.

> Provides more in-depth discussion of various data collection instruments, describes measurement tools and methods, and includes comparison tables for each method that may be of use as you consider various strategies. Also addresses the importance of using multiple measures to compare and contrast, increasing the reliability and validity of data, which is useful in brand promotion.

Dooley, Roger. 2021. "Good Marketers Are Good Observers." Forbes.com. Last modified September 30, 2021. forbes.com/sites/rogerdooley/2021/09/30/good-marketers-are-good-observers/?sh=300530181517.

> "When you observe a customer, you are seeing their actual behavior—not a self-reported and perhaps inaccurate preference or belief." This is a quick read that reinforces the necessity to observe direct customer experience with your brand.

Chapter 6: Identifying and Overcoming Barriers

American Association of School Librarians. 2019. "Appropriate Staffing for School Libraries." Position Statements. Last modified June 22, 2019. ala.org/aasl/advocacy/resources/statements.

> This position statement from AASL underscores the fact that the "success of a school library, no matter how well designed, ultimately depends on the quality and number of personnel responsible for managing the instructional program and the school library's physical and virtual resources." It is a valuable statement from which to construct a rationale for the need for both professionals and para-professionals in the school library.

Jacubowicz, Collette. 2022. "6 Essentials Every School Library Website Needs." *Mrs. J in the Library*. Last modified 2022. mrsjinthelibrary.com/library-website-essentials.

> Using a checklist format with practical tips, "Mrs. J." provides her top six recommendations for what every school library website should have. As a bonus, four additional expert-level extras are included.

Kachel, Deb. 2017. "Advocating for the School Library Budget." *Teacher Librarian* 42, no. 2 (December): 48–50, 63.

> One of the profession's foremost authorities on advocacy posits that a budget plan begins with advocacy and then provides practical advice and suggestions on the development of that plan.

Mandel, Lauren H., and Melissa P. Johnston. 2017. "Evaluating Library Signage: A Systematic Method for Conducting a Library Signage Inventory." *Journal of Librarianship and Information Science* 51, no. 1 (January 15): 150–61. doi.org/10.1177/0961000616681837.

> How much signage is "enough" or "too much"? This study provides a method to conduct a signage inventory and includes a practical worksheet that can be adapted to address factors related to the school library.

Chapter 7: Extreme Makeover

LaGarde, Jennifer. 2020. "BFTP! Keeping Your Library Collection Smelling F.R.E.S.H!" *The Adventures of Library Girl!* (blog). April 30, 2020. librarygirl.net/post/bftp-keeping-your-library-collection-smelling-f-r-e-s-h.

> This updated Jennifer LaGarde blog post provides justification (often needed) for weeding and enhancing school library collections and provides excellent guidelines to "create more inclusive, equitable and culturally responsive school library spaces/collections district wide."

New York City School Library System. 2022. "Diversity Audits." *New York City School Library System Handbook*. Last modified October 17, 2022. nycdoe.libguides.com/librarianguidebook/diversityaudit.

> The excellent NYC School Library System handbook includes a definition of and guide for a diversity audit. "A diversity audit is an inventory of a collection designed to measure the amount of diversity within the collection. It is a tool used to analyze collection data to make sure we include a wide variety of points of view, experiences, and representations within a collection. Reflective practitioners realize it is important, now more than ever, to intentionally, and even aggressively, be working to diversify our collections."

New York City School Library System. 2022. "Weeding." *New York City School Library System Handbook*. Last modified October 17, 2022. nycdoe.libguides.com/librarianguidebook/weeding.

> This helpful resource from the NYC SLS includes a guide for deselecting library material, including a letter for gaining support for weeding, often misunderstood by the school community.

New York State Education Department, Department of Curriculum Instruction. 2020. "NYSED School Library Program Rubric." nysed.gov/curriculum-instruction/nysed-school-library-program-rubric.

> This comprehensive rubric is a helpful self-assessment instrument to support the school library program, facilitating analysis of and reflection on current programs, aiding in the creation of an action plan for developing a school library program that enables students to grow and succeed as readers and learners.

Stripling, Barbara K. 2019. *Empire State Information Fluency Continuum*. School Library Systems Association of New York State. slsa-nys.libguides.com/ifc.

> The Empire State Information Fluency Continuum (ESIFC) enhances collaboration with other educators for information literacy instruction for all learners. It is a customizable scope and sequence and *much* more. It is used by NYS school librarians as well as school librarians in many other states and countries. The ESIFC provides a Pre-K–12 continuum of skills, identification of priority skills for every grade level, and graphic organizer assessments for the priority skills.

Chapter 8: Communications Plan

American Association of School Librarians. 2015. *Toolkit for Promoting School Library Programs*. Chicago, IL: AASL. ala.org/aasl/sites/ala.org.aasl/files/content/aasl issues/toolkits/promo/AASL_Toolkit_Promoting_SLP_033016.pdf.

> An updated version of a seminal publication produced by AASL as part of the ALA @your library campaign. This helpful online version includes messages as well as ideas and strategies for promoting and communicating the value of the school library and school librarian.

American Library Association. n.d. "Frontline Advocacy for School Libraries Toolkit." ala.org/advocacy/frontline-advocacy-school-libraries-toolkit.

> Developed in 2010, this toolkit continues to provide excellent tools for developing an advocacy/marketing plan and messaging on an everyday basis by school library staff and everyone in the school library community.

Doucett, Elisabeth. 2008. *Creating Your Library Brand: Communicating Your Relevance and Value to Your Patrons*. Chicago: ALA.

> This book focuses on defining the brand message and using visuals and other communication tools to deliver the same to various stakeholders. Includes a helpful list of words to "describe your library and what makes it unique."

Thomsett-Scott, Beth C., ed. 2020. *Marketing with Social Media*. 2nd ed. Chicago: ALA Neal-Schuman.

> Though not targeted at school librarians, this book published by ALA's Library and Information Technology Association (LITA) connects school librarians to marketing techniques and reviews of current social media tools to reach critical audiences with tailored and targeted messaging. It is useful for those who have yet begun to use social media for their school libraries and for those who want to improve their current practices. It includes links to online training.

GLOSSARY

brand. A concept or a psychological construct that helps identify a brand in the mind of an individual.

brand barriers. Challenges and impediments that impact positive brand development.

brand behavior. The expectations that people have about the brand based on the experience that they have at points of contact with the brand.

brand collateral. The creative content assets (physical and digital) used to promote and identify the brand.

brand credibility. Positive perception based on trustworthiness and reputation.

brand experience. User engagement and interaction with a brand.

brand identity. Combined design elements and related marketing and merchandizing to present and promote the brand.

brand loyalty. Repeat commitment to the brand based on positive experiences.

brand management. Strategies to increase awareness and understanding of the value of the brand and improve and maintain the brand over time.

brand perception. What individuals believe a brand is, not what the brand says it is.

brand rehabilitation. Rebuilding confidence, trust, and loyalty after a negative event or experience with the brand.

branding. What the brand is known for or wants to be known for; what makes it unique and distinctive.

design elements. Specific name, logo, tagline, color palette, fonts, and the like that create a cohesive and recognizable image.

logo. Symbolic graphic identification or representation of a particular company, organization, individual, product, commodity, or service.

marketing. Strategies and activities designed to promote and increase interest in and awareness of a brand through various communication channels.

merchandizing. The presentation and display of brand products, goods, and services.

name brand. A well-known and widely recognized brand.

persona. A fictional personality; a research-based marketing strategy that helps build understanding of the needs and behaviors of communities served.

rebrand. A change or update of the image or perception of the brand.

service culture. One in which the collective focus is on developing overwhelmingly positive brand relationships with individuals and understanding how and why.

stakeholder. Anyone who is involved with or may be impacted, either directly or indirectly, by the brand.

stickiness. An experience or encounter with the brand that is memorable.

tagline. Memorable phrase or slogan identified with a brand.

target audience. Specific group identified for particular brand messaging.

WORKS CITED

AASL American Association of School Librarians. 2009. *Empowering Learners: Guidelines for School Library Programs.* Chicago, IL: American Association of School Librarians.

———. 2018a. "Definition of an Effective School Library." Position Statements. Last modified November 11, 2018. ala.org/aasl/advocacy/resources/statements.

———. 2018b. *National School Library Standards for Learners, School Librarians, and School Libraries.* Chicago: ALA Editions.

———. 2019a. *Appropriate Staffing for School Libraries.* Position Statements. Last modified June 22, 2019. ala.org/aasl/advocacy/resources/statements.

———. 2019b. *Position Statement on School Library Scheduling.* Last modified June 2019. ala.org/aasl/sites/ala.org.aasl/files/content/advocacy/statements/docs/AASL _Scheduling_Position_Statement.pdf.

———. 2019c. "Role of the School Library." Position Statements. Last modified June 2019. ala.org/aasl/advocacy/resources/statements.

———. 2020. "Instructional Role of the School Librarian." Position Statements. Last modified June 29, 2020. ala.org/aasl/advocacy/resources/statements.

———. 2021. "National School Library of the Year Award Rubric." National School Library of the Year Award. Last modified 2021. ala.org/aasl/sites/ala.org.aasl/files/content/ aaslawards/NSLY_Rubric2021.pdf.

———. 2022. *School Libraries Transform Learning Message Box.* AASL National School Library Standards Portal. standards.aasl.org/project/message-box/.

ALA American Library Association. 2019. "AASL Releases Guide to Develop Inclusive Learners and Citizens." News release. July 30, 2019. ala.org/news/press-releases/ 2019/07/aasl-releases-guide-develop-inclusive-learners-and-citizens.

———. 2021. *Intellectual Freedom Manual.* 10th ed. Chicago, IL: American Library Association.

———. 2022a. *Libraries Transform: The Expert in the School Library.* Last modified June 28, 2022. libguides.ala.org/school-library-expert.

———. 2022b. *Action Toolkit.* Unite Against Book Bans. Last modified 2022. uniteagainst bookbans.org/toolkit/.

———. 2022c. *Libraries Transform: The Expert in the School Library—Communicate Your Expertise.* libguides.ala.org/school-library-expert/communicate-expert.

ALA/AASL American Library Association, and American Association of School Librarians. 2017. "Baltimore County Public Schools Named National School Library Program of the Year." News release. April 26, 2017. ala.org/news/press-releases/2017/04/baltimore-county-public-schools-named-national-school-library-program-year.

———. 2019. "Illinois High School District 214 Named National School Library of the Year." News release. May 2, 2019. ala.org/news/press-releases/2019/05/illinois-high-school-district-214-named-national-school-library-year.

Archimedes. (287–212 BCE) 1957. In Diodorus Siculus, *Library of History, Volume XI: Fragments of Books 21–32.* Translated by F. R. Walton. Loeb Classical Library 409. Cambridge, MA: Harvard University Press.

Barber, Peggy, and Linda K. Wallace. 2010. *Building a Buzz: Libraries and Word-of-Mouth Marketing.* Chicago: American Library Association.

BPL Boston Public Library. 2020. "Facts & Figures." bpl.org/about-us/statistics/.

Brier, David. 2015. "How to Rebrand: 19 Questions to Ask Before You Start." *Successful Brands + Disruptive Strategies* (blog). September 2, 2015. medium.com/successful-brands-disruptive-strategies/how-to-rebrand-19-questions-to-ask-before-you-start-a9604d700baf.

Carlson, Scott. 2007. "An Anthropologist in the Library." *The Chronicle of Higher Education* 53 (50): A26.

Carnegie, Dale. 1981. *How to Win Friends and Influence People.* Revised ed. New York: Simon & Schuster.

Chattenoogan.com. 2020. "Chattanooga Public Library Responds to COVID-19 with Online Cards, Virtual Programs, Mask Production." March 27, 2020. chattanoogan.com/2020/3/27/406633/Chattanooga-Public-Library-Responds.aspx.

Chow, Anthony S., Rebecca J. Morris, Amy Figley, Karla Regan, Samantha Lam, and Jessica Sherard. 2016. "How Usable Are School Library Websites? A Random Sample from All Fifty States." *The Journal of Research on Libraries and Young Adults* 7 (June 10). yalsa.ala.org/jrlya/2016/06/how-usable-are-school-library-websites-a-random-sample-from-all-fifty-states/.

Cockcroft, Marlaina. 2021. "Farewell, Fines: Libraries Eliminate Late Fees." *School Library Journal,* November 18, 2021. slj.com/story/farewell-fines-libraries-eliminate-fate-fees.

Collins, Jim. 2001. *Good to Great.* New York, NY: HarperCollins.

———. 2005. *Good to Great and the Social Sectors: A Monograph to Accompany Good to Great.* Boulder, CO: Jim Collins.

Cooper, Alan, Robert Riemann, and David Cronin. 2007. *About Face: The Essentials of Interaction Design.* 3rd ed. Hoboken, NJ: Wiley.

CPL Chattanooga Public Library. n.d. "4th Floor." chattlibrary.org/4th-floor/.

Dowd, Nancy, Mary Evangeliste, and Jonathan Silberman. 2010. *Bite-Sized Marketing: Realistic Solutions for the Overworked Librarian*. Chicago, IL: American Library Association.

Eichenlaub, Iris. 2019. "Co(mmunity)-Constructed Library." *AASL KQ Blog*. December 6, 2019. knowledgequest.aasl.org/community-constructed-library/.

Eliot, T. S. 1925. "The Hollow Men." All Poetry. allpoetry.com/the-hollow-men.

Ellis, Leanne. 2022. "Upgrading Library Collections: Selecting Books Students Want to Read." *Knowledge Quest*. Last modified October 18, 2022. knowledgequest.aasl.org/upgrading-library-collections-selecting-books-students-want-to-read/#comment -558501.

Gibbons, Sarah. 2018. "Empathy Mapping: The First Step in Design Thinking." Nielsen Norman Group. January 14, 2018. nngroup.com/articles/empathy-mapping/.

Godin, Seth. 2009. "Define: Brand." *Seth's Blog*. December 13, 2009. seths.blog/2009/12/define-brand/.

Goltz, Schlomo "Mo." 2014. "A Closer Look at Personas: A Guide to Developing the Right Ones (Part 2)." *Smashing Magazine*. smashingmagazine.com/2014/08/a-closer-look -at-personas-part-2/.

Goodall, Jane. 2002. "Subject: Jane Goodall, Primatologist and Conservationist." Interview by River Path Associates. *The Daily Summit*. Last modified August 26, 2002. dailysummit.net/says/interview260802.htm.

Harland, Pamela Colburn. 2014. "Kicked Out of the Library." *Pam Librarian—Transforming Traditional Libraries into Thriving Learning Commons* (blog). March 8, 2014. pamlibrarian.wordpress.com/2014/03/08/kicked-out-of-the-library/.

Humphrey, Aaron. 2017. "User Personas and Social Media Profiles." *Persona Studies* 3 (2): 13–20. dx.doi.org/10.21153/ps2017vol3no2art708.

Ibrisevic, Ilma. 2019. "7 Essential Tips for Building a Strong Nonprofit Brand." *Donorbox Nonprofit Blog*. February 9, 2019. donorbox.org/nonprofit-blog/building-a-strong -nonprofit-brand/.

Johns, Sara Kelly. 2015. "'Flipping the Switch' for School Library Advocacy." In *Creative Library Marketing and Publicity: Best Practices*, edited by Robert J. Lackie and M. Sandra Wood, 167–82. Lanham, MD: Roman & Littlefield.

Johnson, Doug. 2013. "Getting Your End of the Year Report Read." *Blue Skunk Blog*. May 29, 2013. doug-johnson.squarespace.com/blue-skunk-blog/2013/5/29/getting-your -end-of-the-year-report-read.html.

———. 2018. "10 Traits of Successful School Librarians." *Blue Skunk Blog*. May 9, 2018. doug-johnson.squarespace.com/blue-skunk-blog/2018/5/9/10-traits-of-successful -school-librarians.html.

Kachel, Debra, and Christie Kaaland. 2021. *School Librarianship: Evolving or Declining? Findings from an IMLS Project*. AASL 2021 National Conference Session, October 22, 2021. AASL Learning Library.

Kaplan, Allison G. 2006. *Benign Neglect: Principals' Knowledge of and Attitudes Towards School Library Media Specialists.* Unpublished doctoral dissertation, University of Delaware.

Keer, Gretchen, and Andrew Carlos. 2015. "The Stereotype Stereotype: Our Obsession with Librarian Representation." *American Libraries* (October 30). americanlibraries magazine.org/2015/10/30/the-stereotype-stereotype/.

Kerby, Mona. 2019. *An Introduction to Collection Development for School Librarians.* 2nd ed. Chicago, IL: ALA/AASL.

Kotter, John, and Holger Rathgeber. 2005. *Our Iceberg Is Melting.* New York, NY: St. Martin's Press.

Kylander, Nathalie, and Christopher Stone. 2012. "The Role of Brand in the Nonprofit Sector." *Stanford Social Innovation Review* (Spring). ssir.org/articles/entry/the_role_of_brand_in_the_nonprofit_sector.

LaGarde, Jennifer. 2011. "5 Things Every School Library Website Should Have." *The Adventures of Library Girl!* (blog). August 9, 2011. librarygirl.net/post/5-things-every-school-library-website-should-have.

Lewis, Melanie. 2020. "Advocating for the School Library through Partnerships." *Knowledge Quest* 49 (1): 46–51.

Liu, Ken. 2016. *The Paper Menagerie and Other Stories.* London, UK: Saga Press.

Lombardi, Vince. n.d. "Famous Quotes by Vince Lombardi." VinceLombardi.com. vincelombardi.com/quotes.html.

Mackley, Allison, and Dustin Brackbill. 2020. "PSLA Believes in Distance Learning." *Knowledge Quest* (blog). April 22, 2020. knowledgequest.aasl.org/psla-believes-in-distance-learning/.

McCoy, Erin. 2018. "Library Signage." Librarian Design Share. Last modified April 5, 2018. librariandesignshare.org/category/library-signage/.

McLuhan, Marshall. 1964. *Understanding Media: The Extensions of Man.* New York, NY: Mentor.

Mead, Margaret. 1972. *Blackberry Winter: My Earlier Years.* New York, NY: Kodansha International.

Moore, Hayleigh. 2020. "The High John Library (1967): Shaping the Future of Libraries as Community Resource Centers." College of Information Studies, iSchool News. February 11, 2020. ischool.umd.edu/news/high-john-library-1967-shaping-future-libraries-community-resource-centers.

Morville, Peter. 2004. "User Experience Design." Semantic Studios. Last modified June 21, 2004. semanticstudios.com/user_experience_design/.

———. n.d. "User Experience Basics." usability.gov/what-and-why/user-experience.html.

Nawaz, Sabina. 2017. "The Problem with Saying 'Don't Bring Me Problems, Bring Me Solutions.'" *Harvard Business Review* (blog). Last modified September 1, 2017.

hbr.org/2017/09/the-problem-with-saying-dont-bring-me-problems-bring-me -solutions.

Pew Research Center. 2021. *Social Media Fact Sheet.* April 7, 2021. pewresearch.org/ internet/fact-sheet/social-media/.

Pink, Daniel H. 2006. *A Whole New Mind. Why Right-Brainers Will Rule the Future.* New York, NY: Riverhead Books.

———. 2012. "Textbook Example of Emotionally Intelligent Signage." *Emotionally Intelligent Signage* (blog). April 2012. danpink.com/2012/04/textbook-example -of-emotionally-intelligent-signage/.

Roys, Nadine K., and Mary E. Brown. 2004. "The Ideal Candidate for Library Media Specialist: Views from School Administrators, Library School Faculty, and MLS Students." *School Library Media Research*, 7. ala.org/aasl/sites/ala.org.aasl/files/ content/aaslpubsandjournals/slr/vol7/SLMR_IdealCandidate_V7.pdf.

Sacco, Christina. 2020. "Chattanooga Library Offers Online Cards, Virtual Programs, Mask Production." *The Pulse* (Chattanooga, TN), March 28, 2020, Local News. http:// www.chattanoogapulse.com/local-news/chattanooga-library-offers-online-cards -virtual-programs-mas/.

Sannwald, Suzanne. 2017. "Practical User Experience Design for School Libraries: 5 Tips for Improving Day-to-Day Life for Your Users . . . and You!" *Knowledge Quest* 45 (5): 38–47.

Seelye, Katharine Q. 2014. "Breaking Out of the Library Mold, in Boston and Beyond." *New York Times*, March 8, 2014, New York edition, A9. nytimes.com/2014/03/08/us/ breaking-out-of-the-library-mold-in-boston-and-beyond.html.

Shannon, Donna M. 2009. "Principals' Perceptions of School Librarians." *School Libraries Worldwide* 15 (2): 1–22. https://scholarcommons.sc.edu/cgi/viewcontent.cgi?article =1010&context=libsci_facpub.

Spector, Robert, and Patrick McCarthy. 2012. *The Nordstrom Way to Customer Service Excellence: The Handbook for Becoming the "Nordstrom" of Your Industry.* 2nd ed. Hoboken, NJ: John Wiley & Sons.

Sullivan, Margaret L. 2013. *Library Spaces for 21st-Century Learners.* Chicago, IL: American Association of School Librarians.

———. 2015. *High Impact School Library Spaces.* Santa Barbara, CA: Libraries Unlimited.

Tetreault, Steve. 2019. "Don't Penalize Students Who Want to Read: Remove Fines." *Knowledge Quest* (blog). September 4, 2019. knowledgequest.aasl.org/dont-penalize -students-who-want-to-read-remove-fines/.

———. 2022. "(Re)Building a School Library, Part 1: The Website." *Knowledge Quest* (blog). April 14, 2022. knowledgequest.aasl.org/rebuilding-a-school-library-part-1 -the-website/.

Toister, Jeff. 2018. "What Exactly Is a Service Culture?" *Inside Customer Service Blog.* May 31, 2018. toistersolutions.com/blog/2018/5/29/what-exactly-is-a-service-culture.

Tripadvisor. 2023. "Top Attractions in Boston." tripadvisor.com/Attractions-g60745
-Activities-Boston_Massachusetts.html.

U.S. Department of Education. n.d. *Access to Reading Materials: Circulation of Children's
Library Materials, by School District.* www2.ed.gov/datastory/bookaccess/index
.html#datanotes.

U.S. Department of Health and Human Services. n.d. *Research-Based Web Design and
Usability Guidelines.* usability.gov/sites/default/files/documents/guidelines_book
.pdf.

U.S. General Services Administration, Technology Transformation Services. n.d. "User
Experience Basics." Usability.gov. usability.gov/what-and-why/user-experience
.html.

Valenza, Joyce Kasman. 2022. "Your Library Website: It's a Destination, Not a Brochure!"
SchoolLibraryNJ. September 5, 2022. schoollibrarynj.libguides.com/Librarians/
websites.

Vogels, Emily A., Risa Gelles-Watnick, and Navid Massarat. 2022. *Teens, Social Media
and Technology 2022.* Pew Research Center, August 10, 2022. pewresearch.org/
internet/2022/08/10/teens-social-media-and-technology-2022.

Ward, Jennifer L. 2010. "Persona Development and Use; or, How to Make Imaginary
People Work for You." In *Proceedings of the 2010 Library Assessment Conference,*
477–83. University of Washington. http://hdl.handle.net/1773/19303.

Welbourne, James. 1972. "Training Urban Information Specialists." In *Libraries and
Neighborhood Information Centers: Papers Presented at an Institute Conducted by
the University of Illinois Graduate School of Library Science October 24–27, 1971,*
edited by Carol L. Kronus and Linda Crowe, 100–09. Champaign-Urbana, IL:
University of Illinois.

Yamauchi, Haruko. 2018. "Urban Information Specialists and Interpreters: An Emerging
Radical Vision of Reference for the People, 1967–1973." *CUNY Academic Works.*
academicworks.cuny.edu/ho_pubs/68/.

Zaugg, Holt, and Scott Rackham. 2016. "Identification and Development of Patron
Personas for an Academic Library." *Performance Measurement and Metrics* 17 (2):
124–33. https://www.emerald.com/insight/content/doi/10.1108/PMM-04-2016
-0011/full/html.

Zipursky, Michael. n.d. "The BEST Way to Get Testimonials from Clients (& How to
Use Them)." Consulting Success. consultingsuccess.com/how-to-get-testimonials
-from-clients.

ABOUT THE AUTHORS

Susan D. Ballard. A former director of Library, Media and Technology, Susan guided her district to AASL National School Library of the Year Award recognition. She has served as an adjunct professor and lecturer in various school librarian preparation programs, published numerous articles in professional and scholarly journals, and edited and contributed to several books. A past president of AASL, the New Hampshire School Library Media Association, and the New England School Library Association, Susan served on the Standards and Guidelines Editorial Board for the *National School Library Standards for Learners, School Librarians, and School Libraries.*

Sara Kelly Johns, an online instructor at the Syracuse University iSchool and a long-time school librarian, is a past president of AASL, the New York Library Association (NYLA), and the Section of School Librarians of NYLA. She received the NYLA Lifetime Achievement Award and the first AASL Social Media Superstar Advocacy Ambassador Award. Active in ALA Council and ALA committees, Johns was a member of the Implementation Task Force for the *National School Library Standards for Learners, School Librarians, and School Libraries.* She has written articles for several school library publications and contributed chapters for various books.

Susan and Sara were coeditors with Dorcas Hand of the ALA LibGuide entitled *Libraries Transform: The Expert in the School Library.*

INDEX

Printed in the USA
CPSIA information can be obtained
at www.ICGtesting.com
JSHW060705130924
69666JS00002B/10

9 780838 938706